DRAMA IMPROVISED

By the same author:

Books:

Choreographing the Stage Musical (with M. Sunderland)
Drama Improvised
Drama in the Cathedral (Churchman)
How to Study Modern Drama (Macmillan)
Masterguide to *A Midsummer Night's Dream* (Macmillan)
Masterguide to *The Tempest* (Macmillan)

Plays:

Beowulf (French/Clark)
The Ingoldsby Legends
The Inside Story (Miller/Clark)
The Midlands Mysteries (With D. Sugano)
One Child at a Time
The Parting of Friends
Snow White and the Seven Dwarfs (Miller/Clark)
Troilus and Criseyde (With M. Herzog)
Ulysses (French)
Mothers and Daughters (French)

Drama Improvised

A source book for
teachers and therapists

Kenneth Pickering

Director of Studies
The Institute for the Arts in Therapy and Education, London.

J. Garnet Miller
Theatre Arts Books

Copyright © Kenneth Pickering 1997

First published by J. Garnet Miller Limited in 1957
Second Edition published in 1997 by

J. Garnet Miller in the UK
A Division of Cressrelles Publishing Company Limited
10 Station Road Industrial Estate, Colwall WR13 6RN

Theatre Arts Books in the USA
An Imprint of Routledge, New York
29 West 35th Street, New York, NY 10001-2299

Radical Will Copyright © Claudia Leaf 1997
First Published by J. Garnet Miller in 1997

A CIP record is available from the British Library
Library of Congress CIP data is available

United Kingdom ISBN: 0 85343 612 6
United States of America ISBN: 0 87830 066 X

Printed and bound in Great Britain by BPC Wheatons Ltd

Contents

For all my students:

Past, present and future.

Acknowledgements

I wish to express my particular debt to my tutor, Barbara Hood; to my colleagues, Dr. Michael Hinton, Bob Murphy, Rodney Wood and Dr. David Male, for their guidance at key moments in my work; to Margot Sunderland at *The Institute for the Arts in Therapy and Education* and to Dr. John Caputo at *Gonzaga University* for the opportunities to rethink my work; and to Meagan Louden and Jason Bowler for permission to use their play as an example.

My sincere thanks also to Sara Herr Waldroup in Faculty Services at *Gonzaga University* and to Claudia Leaf of the *Channel Theatre Company* for permission to use her script.

Kenneth W. Pickering,
Canterbury, 1997

Introduction

Almost twenty-five years have elapsed since the first publication of this book which was intended as an accessible and inexpensive source of ideas for drama teachers. During that time, the entire system which produced that generation of drama teachers has largely been dismantled and drama itself, once almost a symbol and focus of creative education, has been marginalised by more utilitarian views and stifled under a weight of definable goals, assessable skills and so-called vocational considerations.

The training of drama teachers now rarely takes place in a situation where theatre skills and insights into child development can fertilise each other. Even the notion as to what constitutes Drama-in-Education has become detached from the study of theatre or the acquisition of theatre skills such as improvisation. In 1979, Gavin Bolton's *Towards a Theory of Drama in Education* and Francis Hilton's *The Vocabulary of Educational Drama* seemed to have established the place of drama in the curriculum with a reassuring firmness, and in the same year, Betty Jane Wagner produced her tribute to the innovative and inspiring work of Dorothy Heathcote - *Drama as a Learning Medium*.

The following five or so years saw the publication of similar books and of Keith Johnstone's *Impro*, one of the most widely used books on improvisation. Although subsequent years produced a stream of source books and studies of the use of drama as a tool subject, it is now possible to view those years as an ever increasing struggle for justification and survival for the kind of play-based drama that had stimulated the first edition of this book.

During those years, too, although drama teachers were establishing themselves as heads and leaders of Creative Arts and integrated faculties in schools, the position of their subject was being steadily undermined, so that it returned to being an adjunct of English or an after-hours activity which tested professional loyalty to the limit.

In the past twenty-five years also, the information explosion has impacted upon almost every facet of life. Our children and young people have unparalleled access to information from a huge variety of technological sources. Music can be personally administered to the ears, whilst the press of a button creates visual games. Human beings pass ever increasing numbers of years of their lives in front of television screens and the use of books as a source of wonderment, imagination and information is now receding with the advance of the CD-ROM. More alarmingly, perhaps, society seems to have absorbed the values of the technocrats and the market place. The only charters we seem to value now are those designed to protect our consumerism.

Where, in all this drive for efficiency, productivity and information, is there a place for wisdom, or compassion or imagination? Where, in fact, is there room for our humanity? Is it any wonder that the theatre is viewed with suspicion by our leaders unless it is simply a packaged piece of technological wizardry that challenges nothing. Is it at all surprising that the truly oppressed find a voice in the theatre of Boal or Brecht? Is it remarkable that improvised drama has become a means of protest, of challenge and of deep questioning in our society?

The result of many of the changes I have indicated is that teachers no longer have the opportunity, motivation or energy to use the techniques of improvised drama and that many have never acquired the skill in the first place. Yet I believe that it is possible to demonstrate that the need is as great as ever and that a new edition of this book can make a useful contribution to the rediscovery of one of the most creative strands of modern education. Furthermore, there are now new and challenging fields for the techniques with which this book deals: these form part of this initial discussion of the value and foundation of a type of drama which does not originate from a script.

Drama in Childhood

Memories of childhood almost invariably include vivid recollections of dramatic games. In her sensitive portrait of life in a late nineteenth-century home in London, Molly Hughes recalls the play-making that occurred around Christmas time:

"Tom and Dym kept going to Upper Street to get stationery, cards and presents from the shops. Charles spent his time in painting home-made Christmas cards. Midday dinner was a noisy buzz of comparing notes on the morning's doings, and having a look at what Charles had produced. The afternoons were generally given up to the preparation of our annual play.

It fell to Tom to devise the plot, and to Charles, the Bully Bottom of the family, fell nearly everything else. He took the part of the villain or the comic washer-woman, and kept thinking up ideas for improving the parts of others. He taught me how to act when I wasn't speaking, how to listen with agitation, how to do 'by-play', how to swoon and once, even, how to die. Dym was usually the hero, a bit stiff, but always dignified. Barnholdt had to be given a part with little to say, because, however willing, he could not be relied on to remember the words, or improvise other ones. He would be a coachman or a footman, or perhaps only the scene-shifter. What he really loved was to be the policeman, coming in at the crisis with a "'Ere, what's all this?'", pulling out his notebook, wetting his thumb and, taking people's addresses. He knew his stuff for this perfectly, but it wouldn't always fit into melodrama.

Tom, to my great comfort, was prompter, and saved me from many a breakdown when I was swamped with nervousness. I didn't actually forget my words, but I should have done if Tom hadn't stood by smiling at me behind the screen.

Christmas Eve was the day we liked best. The morning was a frenzied rush for last rehearsals, last posting of cards, last buying of presents. My father came home early, laden with parcels. The tea table was resplendent with bonbons (crackers), sweets and surprise cakes with icing on the top and three-penny-bits inside. The usual 'bread and butter first' rule was set aside, and we all ate and talked and laughed to our heart's content.

Then followed the solemn ascent to study for the play. The boys had borrowed chairs from the bedrooms, and placed them in two rows: the front (stalls) for father, mother, and any aunt, uncle, or visitor who happened to be there, and the back (pit) for the servants, who attended with much gigglement."

I have quoted this passage at length because it captured the sense of fantasy, absorption and imagination which is involved with creating drama. There are similar passages in Kay William's biography of Richmal Crompton, the creator of *Just William*, in Henry Warren's *A Boy in Kent*, where the magic of a puppet theatre is recalled and, of course, in Louisa M. Alcott's, albeit fictional, *Little Women*. Although all these books preserve a tradition of child-initiated drama with an overtly theatrical form, they all have in common a strong improvisatory element; and it is quite remarkable just how many biographies and autobiographies record the impact of involvement with play-making as a profound developmental influence in early life.

Many children construct their own inner dramas, often inventing characters and engaging them in dialogue. In his biography of the British dramatist Harold Pinter, Michael Billington tells how the playwright recalls "creating a small body of imaginary friends" in his back garden when he was eight or nine. With these invisible friends, he would talk aloud and invent a total fantasy life. Many of us must have had a similar experience resulting in an urge to "create characters and exchange dialogue". With this richness of imaginative life, it is hardly surprising that Pinter was soon to give outstanding, youthful school performances as Macbeth and Romeo and develop into a dramatist with an astonishing ear for dialogue and a vivid sense of inner landscape.

The ability to play creatively and to give that play some kind of form lies at the root of children's personal development. That play needs to be expansive, imaginative, noisy, physical and experimental. It enables children to explore their world and the rôles within it. It enables them to devise rules and experience ritual, to engage their whole being in a response to what they see and feel about the world and to stop the game when they have had enough.

Recently, I was watching a skilled facilitator leading a group activity and was moved by her injunction to the group to "be powerful, be playful." In discussion with her afterwards, she asserted the importance of play in the lives of her own children and said that of course her ten year old daughter still had her 'dressing-up box'. We live in a world where, all too often, play stops abruptly and work begins. We even forget how to play and yet the word 'play' itself is a constant reminder to us that drama, which is capable of exploring every facet of the human condition in the most profound way, is an extension of what is so precious to us as children.

Drama and Adolescence

With the approach of adolescence, the need to make sense of the world and to develop inter-personal skills through types of play is even more acute and yet it is precisely at this time that our educational systems seem to stifle such activity. In the first edition of this book, I deliberately showed illustrations of teenagers and senior pupils taking part in improvised drama. I maintain the belief that adolescents, whose developing personalities are full of emotional and social complexities and who frequently feel ill at ease with themselves and their bodies, can find in the drama lesson just the release and guidance they need. Introspective natures can be gently and painlessly nurtured.

DRAMA IMPROVISED

The awe with which such great drama teachers as Peter Slade and Dorothy Heathcote were held was often due to the remarkable level of enthusiasm, involvement and serious artistry that they achieved with apparently resistant teenagers, demonstrating beyond doubt that improvised drama was an activity of value to all age groups. Furthermore, it is in the later years of schooling that students engage in production work and in Theatre Studies. Work in improvised drama can play a valuable part in improving students' technical skill as actors and deepen their sense of characterisation.

Drama Therapy

Drama has always had therapeutic potential. A catharsis we might feel when witnessing a great tragedy, for example, may be both healing and cleansing. As drama techniques were acquired by teachers after the Second World War, these skills were gradually extended to be used by a whole variety of groups other than those found in conventional schools. Drama has been found to be of help to those with disabilities of all kinds, to be useful in certain forms of training where 'rôle-play' had become a widely employed technique and as a potent treatment for the emotionally disturbed.

Nothing, perhaps, illustrates more clearly the spiritual bankruptcy and imaginative impoverishment of our current generation, with its endless talk of a return to old 'values', more clearly than the number of people who have turned to the Creative Arts therapies to find some meaning and structure in life. Drama has played a major rôle in this development and drama therapy has sometimes claimed an exclusiveness of techniques which is not entirely justified. Several text and source books of drama therapy are, in fact, little more than regurgitation of games and ideas long used by teachers in schools. To claim a specificity for them in a therapeutic context is hardly justified.

However, even such sophisticated drama therapy techniques as Moreno's 'psycho-drama' or Augusto Boal's 'Forum theatre' both presuppose some skill in improvised drama on the part of the group facilitator and, indeed, of the participants. There are a number of specific approaches which have been found particularly effective in therapy. For these reasons there is now a section of this book which offers suggestions for use with therapy groups. But activities outlined in other sections of the book may also be helpful in this work. It is significant that the confidence of practitioners in this field has grown to the extent that their work is now described as 'dramatherapy'.

Improvisation and the Theatre

Improvisation is probably the oldest theatre technique in the world, but it is only since the Second World War that it has begun to be solidified into something of a system. Stanislavsky established the foundations for more recent uses of improvisation by his insistence that actors created an imaginative life for their characters outside the boundaries of the script. Improvised theatre games have now become common currency in developing skills of focus, concentration, imagination and spontaneity. Playwrights like Mike Leigh and the resident writers in small-scale theatre companies frequently use improvisation as a mean of devising an entire play.

At one time, there seemed to be an easy cross-fertilisation between education and the theatre, particularly when the training of drama teachers was closely linked with theatre schools and courses and when Theatre-in-Education companies were frequent visitors to schools. With the use of improvised drama in so many contexts and the gradual demise of arts provision, it has become too easy for improvisation to lose its theatrical roots. However much we may use improvisation as a tool for learning or therapy we must never forget that it is essentially a mode of spontaneous play-making and that it has within it an element of 'performance'.

Working with Groups

Before embarking on drama work involving improvisation, which necessarily demands considerable freedom, it is important for the teacher or leader to establish some rules so that everyone feels comfortable with their sense of control. It might be agreed that at a certain given signal everyone stops what they are doing and listens for further suggestions or instruction, and that once a small group has completed its work it continues to discuss and reflect on the work while the other groups complete. A pre-arranged signal that tells everyone to turn their attention to the teacher or leader may seem petty and stifling of creativity but it is, in fact, a simple framework to ensure that the interventions from the person conducting the session help to move the work forward and establish a good working relationship.

A skilled leader will attempt to watch the entire working group, constantly commenting, praising, encouraging and advising and watching for discomfort or difficulty. It is a useful principle to try to find something over which to enthuse in every session, even if this is a small detail or an achievement by a diffident member of the class or group. Enthusiasm is infectious and groups quickly respond to the genuine interest and concern of the teacher.

Teacher in Rôle

There are many modes by which a teacher or leader can both stimulate and provoke the creation of a drama with a group. One of the most effective methods is for the teacher to adopt a rôle in the drama itself, often initiating a whole train of imaginative thought. This particular technique was demonstrated brilliantly by three teachers involved in the making of a training video for the London and East Anglian Board's G.C.S.E. examination in drama.

One teacher, who had spent some time with her class considering the events in *Hamlet*, entered the drama studio in the rôle of one of the servants at Elsinore with the words,

"You'll never guess what Hamlet has done now!" The group, responding, asked "What?", to which the teacher replied, "Gone to his mother in her bedroom and showed her the picture of his dead dad!" Making it clear that all the group members were, in fact, other servants in the court, the teacher then constructed small group dramas in which servants overheard conversations between Hamlet, Gertrude and Claudius or met up with courtiers who were returning from a period away. Whenever the drama appeared to flag, the teacher injected new pieces of news or challenged the group to action.

A second teacher on the video announced himself as "from the Council" and told an imaginary family that they must leave their home. A third teacher took the rôle of the organiser of an expedition and continued to intervene throughout the resultant drama to move the action forward or refine some of the thinking of the group.

Many teachers have found this way of working to be highly effective, ever since Dorothy Heathcote breezed into classrooms and on teachers' courses in a whole variety of rôles. However, like so many other aspects of drama teaching this approach requires skill and care. I well remember watching one teacher try to create a drama of medieval life in which she adopted the rôle of a blind beggar and very quickly lost control of the situation!

Warm-ups

Readers may be surprised not to find a specific section of this book devoted to 'warm-ups', which have become so much a feature of group drama teaching. The omission stems from my observation that these activities are too frequently seen in isolation and may achieve little beyond initial amusement. Limbering up, freeing the voice and imagination, encouraging loss of inhibition can all be achieved by using activities which lead to further, more complex work. Therefore, many of the suggestions in this book may be used as warm-ups without the sense that they serve only an initiating purpose.

1

Working as Individuals

A considerable number of aims and values have been claimed for work variously described as 'Educational' or 'Creative' Drama and many of these have been extended to Drama Therapy. Perhaps it is not an outrageous simplification to suggest that drama with an improvisational basis embraces three main areas:

1) Opportunities for expression and creativity which help the growing personality and enrich the imaginative life, thus enabling personal and social growth

2) Freeing the body and mind and voice for a fuller, better life and for the arts of the theatre

3) Opportunities for examining human behaviour and for exploring reactions and motives which contribute to the creation of a 'character'.

In the types of lessons and sessions envisaged in this book such broad aims may be narrowed into a number of very specific goals and these may be as diverse as 'overcoming shyness', 'exploring the idea of tolerance', 'feeling at ease with

1

moving the body' or even 'falling over in a play without hurting oneself'. Teachers and group leaders may well have to shift their aims as a session develops: their intervention in the work of the individual or group will invariably be a response to what begins to unfold or to some kind of block or stagnation which inhibits the exploration from moving forward. The important compromise is to have very clear aims and a number of specific strategies for achieving them, coupled with considerable flexibility as to the pace and direction of the session and a readiness to respond to what emerges from the participants.

Because it is hoped that users of this book will come from various teaching and leading situations I shall refer to the time during which the work takes place as 'the session'. This can stand for the lesson or workshop or whatever more precise title is appropriate. I shall refer to the participants as 'students' simply because, in every situation with which this book deals, some learning is envisaged. I realise that 'students' may seem an inappropriate name for children of seven or eight years of age or for a group of adults with emotional difficulties, but if we believe that some genuine learning is possible through improvised drama the label should not be too difficult to accept. I shall refer to the participants as 'the group', which can stand for 'the class' or whatever collective is comfortable for the reader.

It is useful to begin with the group improvising as individuals. This remains as true for starting a session as for embarking on drama work with a new group. The following ideas, therefore, can serve as 'warm-up' exercises for a session or for the type of work that may constitute the main body of a session with a new group. Inexperienced students often find group co-operation difficult in the initial stages and young children are often too egocentric to make elaborate group work feasible.

Solo improvisations move towards some of the aims mentioned earlier. The emphasis initially is on bodily expression of simple and sometimes amusing ideas gradually moving towards elements of characterisation. Students should be encouraged to forget the rest of the group and to focus entirely on their own, individual response by making a small space in the

2

room exclusively theirs. Although some of the ideas suggested here may seem outlandish they have, in fact, proved effective with groups ranging from children with learning difficulties to sophisticated senior students. The way in which they are presented will determine the nature of the work produced.

Exercise A

The group are invited to imagine that they are some of the following objects. They must be given only a few seconds on each example and must change immediately to the next. As they grow more experienced they can take turns at thinking of new subjects. The exact use of these suggestions will depend on the age of the students: whereas a lesson with a young group could be based entirely on solo improvisation, with a group of teenagers it could precede a play rehearsal.

More experienced students may enjoy representing various objects, one at a time, in front of the remainder of the group; and as a test of their success it is frequently rewarding for the object to be kept secret and guessed by the audience. This can be done either by the leader writing the names of the objects on pieces of paper to be drawn from a hat or by the participants thinking of objects for themselves.

Use the following objects:
Front wheel of a car; beam engine, or some large machine part; chewing-gum being chewed or stuck to the ground & being pulled up; bubble-gum; blade of grass in the wind; flower before & after watering; cash dispenser; punch-ball; piece of wire being bent; walking toy; crane; tent on a windy day; arm/rocking/swivel-chair; clock mechanism; weighing machine (see N.F. Simpson, *One Way Pendulum*); pneumatic drill; tree: oak, poplar, willow; plant: ivy, flytrap, cactus; tennis ball; bow being fired; firework: rocket, jumping cracker, whiz-bang, roman candle, damp fire-work; smoke; sprinkler on a garden hose; animal: penguin, seal, gorilla, ostrich; cat: stalking, washing, lying in the sun, playing with a mouse; sea lapping on the beach, breaker; pair of shears; puppet on a string

3

or Punch and Judy; ball of plasticine being rolled into a 'sausage'; bridge; robot; statue of: famous general, great athlete, statesman, sphinx, Assyrian King; painting of: saint, great headmaster, courtier; bulldozer; butter melting; pair of compasses; starfish, crab, jellyfish, a fish caught on a hook; three-legged stool, a table; balloon or tyre being inflated; caterpillar, spider, butterfly.

Exercise B

Occupational themes may be treated in a similar way to the preceding list with the added development of building a character. As the group gains experience they try to visualise their character in other situations. For example, if the group is asked to be a hairdresser, a commentary to help the group might run: "Imagine you are a hairdresser - try to think how old you are - what your home and family are like - what sort of person you are. Let me see you asleep in bed - waking up - getting ready for work - opening the shop. Now you are cutting someone's hair - perhaps a teenage boy's or a young child who will not sit still. Now here's a bad-tempered old gentleman who wants a shampoo. It's lunchtime - closing time - it's evening, what are you doing?"

The applications of this type of work to the scripted play are valuable. Students should be encouraged to imagine the characters they are studying in varied situations not mentioned in the text. For a full treatment of this idea, see Stanislavsky's *Creating A Rôle*.

For all of these examples a supply of chairs is useful:

Road worker - with various mechanical and hand tools; pilot; bill poster; racing driver; window-cleaner on a ladder or 'cradle'; hairdresser; surveyor; anti-aircraft gunner; blacksmith; traffic warden; instrumentalist: double bass, drums, harp, organ, trombone; sculptor; surgeon; barmaid; street vendor; climber; fairground stall-holder; photographer: Victorian and modern; carpenter; waiter or waitress; miner; composer or poet; diver; hunter; mechanic; crane driver; dentist; butcher;

model; cabin steward or stewardess; monk; hypnotist; conjurer; astronaut; coxswain of a lifeboat; sword swallower; fireeater; Indian Yogi; fish & chip shop owner; truck driver.

Exercise C

The simple portrayal of occupations leads naturally to a desire for a plot. This can be provided by a running commentary whilst the group responds. This is one method of acting out a story, as will be seen in a later section. It is important for the leader to watch the group carefully and adjust the speed, tone and wording of the commentary accordingly.

I vividly recall taking part in a session run by the great drama teacher Peter Slade, who achieved so much in the postwar years in Britain and whose book *Child Drama* remains a classic source of inspiration and ideas. Slade took us on a magical journey simply by challenging us to follow his narrative and flesh out ideas and incidents as they arose in our imaginations. As we worked, he played soft music and the level of concentration and involvement was astonishing.

Inevitably, some years later, Slade had his detractors and his technique was sometimes unkindly dubbed the "Voice of God" technique. In the hands of poor imitators of Slade it was, perhaps, nothing more than a heavily guided fantasy that ignored the levels of social learning with which educational drama was increasingly being charged. However, 'guided fantasy' has become part of the normal work of many arts therapies and what Slade had grasped was a technique of dramatic narrative that Brecht did not hesitate to use.

Take, for instance, the following passage from Bertolt Brecht's *The Caucasian Chalk Circle* and consider the dramatic technique being employed. **Grusha** performs the actions as the **Story Teller** describes them:

The Story Teller

Grusha walks a few steps toward the child and bends over it

. . . she went back for one more look at the child.
Only to sit with him for a moment or two,
Only till someone should come,
Its mother, perhaps, or anyone else.

Leaning on a trunk she sits facing the child

Only till she would have to leave, for the danger was too
great,
The city was full of flame and crying.

*The light grows dimmer, as though evening and night
were coming on*

Terrible is the seductive power of goodness!

*Grusha now settles down to watch over the child
through the night*

. . . A long time she sat with the child
Till evening came, till night came, till dawn came.
Too long she sat, too long she saw
The soft breathing, the little fists,
Till towards morning the temptation grew too strong
And she rose, and bent down and, sighing, took the child
And carried it off.

Too often we forget that drama and improvisation are
concerned with telling stories and the following ideas enable
students to respond to and create their own narratives.

1) You are in a submarine. Suddenly, you realise all is not
well. You look through the periscope and see that a giant squid
is holding on. You order the submarine to surface. You struggle
through the conning tower with a harpoon and walk slowly
along the deck which is being lashed by fierce waves. A tentacle

wraps round you and you struggle and cut it with a knife. After a fierce duel, you are able to plunge in the harpoon and return exhausted to the ladder. (Based on Jules Verne's *20,000 Leagues Under the Sea*.)

2) You are in bed in a small room at the top of a large house. As you lie in bed, you suddenly remember that you have left something valuable downstairs. Get up quietly and put on your slippers. It is very cold - quickly you go out on to the landing. You try to avoid noise but a floorboard creaks. Your slippers are loose and you stub your toe going downstairs. Every sound makes you start: someone snoring, a clock chiming. At last you arrive downstairs and find your treasure (pay great attention to opening doors, etc.). On the way back, you enter the wrong room - what happens? Sheer relief when you do arrive in the right place. (Based on *The Pickwick Papers*, Chapter 22 - with older students use the original story.) There are also many other possible variations.

3) You wake one morning and find the sun pouring into the room. You look out of the window and see a huge balloon on the lawn. Rush downstairs and investigate. You grasp the rope and it lifts you high in the air - you are sailing among the clouds looking down. At last the balloon lands - perhaps in a jungle or in the sea - struggle to a clearing or dry land. You find you are in a strange land - possibly Lilliput, and you have some of Gulliver's adventures.

4) You go out of the house one morning, the wind is blowing strongly. You walk to the sea and jump from the sea wall to the beach. As you walk down the shingle, you are facing the wind - spray is showering you. Turn round and lean against the wind. Now pick up flat stones and skim them into the waves. The tide is coming in, so you scramble up the beach and run home with the wind behind you. In the hall of your house you stand gasping with your face wet and the blood tingling in your veins.

5) It is a very warm day and you are enjoying a relaxed stroll along a tree-lined road eating an ice-cream. Looking up, you see a kitten, obviously terrified, on a branch of a tree. You

fetch a ladder and, although it is very heavy, you manage to manoeuvre it into position but, having climbed the ladder you find you can only just reach the kitten. With great difficulty you rescue it and take it to your home.

6) The snow is lying deep and the car you have to drive to work has been standing outside your house all night. You walk gingerly down the path: the milkman is in trouble - the rear wheels of his van are spinning so you go to his aid. You remove the snow from your car's windscreen and spray it with de-icing fluid. You now try to start the car, but without success. Take the starting handle and crank the engine, when at last it fires, run and jump in before it stops again. (It's a very old car!)

7) You have been marching across a desert for days and have run out of water, your feet and tongue are blistered. At last water is sighted ahead, but not content with drinking it you fall into it. (Or use *King Solomon's Mines*, Chapter 6, or *The Rime of the Ancient Mariner*.)

8) You are waiting at a bus stop in the pouring rain late one evening. The bus seems a long time coming, there are several false alarms but eventually it appears. You raise your arm to stop it, but it goes past, splashing you - it was the last bus! There is nothing for it but to walk home, so you plod wearily homeward. When you arrive, cold, tired and hungry, you switch on a fire, cook some baked beans, or some other meal that appeals to you, and sink contentedly into a chair and eat.

9) On an expedition with a friend you come to a river or gully that can only be crossed by a tree trunk. You go first and nearly slip off twice but eventually reach the other side, only to find that you have to persuade your friend to follow you and that he will not come unless you go back and help him across.

10) You are a tiger hunting for prey. After wandering hopelessly through the long grass you finally catch a scent and following it you find a deer. You approach, crouch, spring and catch your prey. (Or a cat hunting a mouse.)

11) As you walk by the river in the cool evening of a summer's day you notice a canoe tied up. You decide to hire the canoe, so pay the boat-house keeper and, with difficulty, climb

in. You paddle downstream and come to a low and awkwardly narrow bridge. Now relax, lie back and trail your fingers in the water. Suddenly you feel a shudder - the boat has stuck in the mud: you begin to panic and eventually fall into the stream. (Try also H. G. Wells's, *The History of Mr. Polly*, Ch. 9, Part III.)
12) Near a cliff top you hear a cry for help. Crawl on your stomach to the edge and look over, it is a dizzy height but you see a young child trapped on a ledge below. You try to reach him or her by climbing down, but your nerves and strength fail you. Fetch a rope and eventually haul the person to safety. (Use blocks, tables or desk tops for this.)

A second type of running commentary can draw on material with which the group is already familiar and may be based on a story or section of a story or on some other form of documentary material that the group has already examined. In schools where Integrated Studies or Combined Arts projects are undertaken the material being used may well have been introduced by another teacher in an earlier session, and where teachers are involved with more than one subject they may wish to draw on material used in other lessons such as History or Social Studies.

Some of the ideas suggested here derive from Greek mythology because the myths deal with so many archetypal situations and engrossing narratives. A good source book of such myths is invaluable for drama teachers but, in a situation of increasing multi-culturalism, it is important for teachers to explore the myths and legends of the backgrounds of all their students. Native American and Norse myths are rich sources of drama and there are equally exciting stories in the legends of Central Europe, the Indian subcontinent or Turkey to name but a few.

The use of part of a story or other work already known to the group may well form the basis of a much more extensive group project. The leader might read to the group in preparation and then a piece of improvised work might emerge from an initial running commentary approach. Some of this might be further polished and several solo improvisations developed into scenes of a more structured play. 'Casting' can take place after everyone in the group has experienced acting out the various rôles.

For example, the story of Ulysses passing the Sirens' Rock might at first be narrated, after which the cast can be chosen: "You are the crew of the ship preparing to embark, loading on food and water. Now set sail, some are rowing, it is hard work, you have to plug your ears. Now you are Ulysses, you hear the Sirens singing, you are being tied to the mast; you are straining to get free. Now you are a Siren, etc."

13) You are Perseus approaching the Gorgon. You are an unfortunate man turned to stone.

14) You are Hercules: a) cleaning the stables by diverting a river through them; b) holding up the Heavens for Atlas; c) slaying the Hydra. (See Thomas Bulfinch's *The Age of Fable*, or any source book of Greek myths.)

15) King Arthur drawing Excalibur from the Stone or Sir Bedivere throwing the sword into the lake.

16) Simon meeting 'The Lord of the Flies' or Ralph being hunted. (William Golding, *The Lord of the Flies*.)

17) Sherlock Holmes grappling with Moriarty on a precipice or investigating a crime.

18) John Unger walking or taking a bath. (Fitzgerald, *Diamond As Big As the Ritz*.)

19) The frog trying to make herself as big as an ox. (*Aesop's Fables*.)

20) Entering Narnia through the wardrobe.

21) Gaspar Ruiz with a cannon on his back, work in pairs with a gunner. (Joseph Conrad, *Gaspar Ruiz*.)

22) Beowulf with Grendel. Grendel's mother.

23) An Astronaut: a) donning a space suit; b) ascending to the capsule; c) in position for the countdown; d) walking in space; e) giving a radio account of what you can see.

24) You are sitting nervously in the pavilion waiting to bat. A wicket falls and your turn comes to face a very fast

bowler, you go through all the usual rituals, but you are bowled out on the second ball, so you must return dejectedly to the pavilion. (Use any other sequence in a sporting event, perhaps based on a newspaper report.)

25) You are the hero of a 'Western': a) entering a saloon; b) showing you are quick on the draw; c) grappling with three attackers in a fist-fight.

26) You are either a great scientist, inventor or explorer making a discovery you have learnt about in History, Geography or Science.

27) You are: King Canute; William the Conqueror landing; Lady Jane Grey; or Queen Elizabeth.

28) You are: a Roman taking a bath or putting on a Toga; a Greek in a pentathlon; a courtly person in Restoration times; a Red-Coat.

Exercise D

Moving on various surfaces in different clothes

The process whereby the body and voice become responsive instruments to the demands of rôle and characterisation is extremely complex and may take some time to develop in students. Age, status, physique, exhaustion, mood and clothes will affect movement as will context, the nature of the surface on which movement is to take place or the ability to see or feel. Creating a character may begin with the acquisition of some physical characteristic or the wearing of some distinctive article of dress. I am reminded of a great actress who said, "I always begin with the feet and I find that the rest will follow."

The following ideas focus attention on small details but they will exercise the imagination as well.

1) You are walking barefoot on: marble; shingle; soft carpet; a pole; a wet, slippery floor; sand (very hot or damp); the sea-bed, gradually getting deeper.

2) You are walking through: mud, wearing Wellingtons; dry leaves; brambles and ferns; snow, wearing boots; long grass; a vegetable garden.

3) You are walking: over stepping-stones; ice on a pond; lush turf; among rock pools; along a narrow ledge; on duck-boards through mud; on planks over an asbestos roof.

4) You are wearing: trainers; hob-nail or jack-boots; ballet shoes; a plaster-cast on one foot; platform or heeled shoes.

5) You are dressed in: flowing robes; Victorian dress; military uniform; circus costume; an academic gown; Regency dress, with lace cuffs; beach wear; a space suit.

6) You are carrying a: rolled umbrella and briefcase; rifle; fan; cane; baton; sword or spear; heavy shopping basket.

7) You are riding in or on a: large motor cycle; train with steamed up windows; sports car; Rolls Royce; vintage car; stagecoach; pony and trap; hobby horse; speedboat; yacht in various weather conditions; tumbril; restaurant car; underground train in the rush hour; lift.

8) You are: water-ski-ing; wind-surfing; para-gliding.

Examples such as these can be extended to group work, such as you are in a lift full of people which breaks down - show the reaction of the inmates.

Exercise E

This section is an extension of *Exercises B* and *D* and is intended for more experienced groups.

1) Show by your whole body and facial movements that you are a: escaped prisoner; poet; attendant in a Turkish bath; ward sister; referee; sergeant-major; commissionaire; driving instructor; umpire; Victorian father; a cheer-leader.

2) Explore a situation in which you show: anger; terror; pride; relaxation; boredom; impatience; amusement.

In this last group it should be noted that students should never be asked to portray emotion without motivation. The leader should work out a sequence to justify the emotion. Thus 'terror' in practice might be: "You are walking home at night along a dark alley and you become aware that somebody is following you."

More complex pieces can involve detailed knowledge of costume and period movement: "You are a medieval princess dressed in a long houppelande and a steeple hennin. You walk through the castle to make a request to the queen. As you enter the throne room you make a deep curtsey and plead for mercy (you have been imprisoned). Or "It is fayre day in the medieval village. you are a jester or tumbler wearing a short paltock, doublet and parti-coloured hose.

Exercise F

Change the chair

Most rooms used for drama will have a supply of chairs and these can be remarkably useful extensions of the body and imagination. A chair can not only represent itself but can also be transformed in the imagination into a whole range of other kinds of chair or into completely different objects. The game suggested here can be used on its own or in conjunction with many of the ideas contained in this chapter. Each student takes a chair and sits on it. Students are then challenged to show how the chair has changed by the way they react to it.

1) Change the chair into a: dentist's chair; throne; piano stool; driving seat; armchair; hairdresser's chair; chair in a waiting room; chair in which you are being interrogated.

The next stage is to change the chair by its usage into another object. The leader can either suggest ideas initially and then, on the word 'change', the group responds or the students can be asked to establish the change of object from the start.

2) Turn the chair into a: wheelbarrow; anti-aircraft gun; musical instrument; fireplace; wide window ledge or sill; the underneath of a car; narrow tunnel; diving board.

2

Introducing an Audience

The sharing and showing of work can be a valuable part of improvised drama, although process is almost invariably more important than product. Some work will benefit from the kind of shaping that is involved in showing what began as a spontaneous piece, but teachers and leaders will be quick to see the inherent dangers of putting students in an actor-audience situation. Exhibitionists will be in their element, whereas shy members of the group, who may well have benefited enormously from their involvement in the work up to this stage, will be in torment. Some may be so embarrassed that they refuse to take part or retreat into cliché or foolery. A relaxed working atmosphere will, in fact, allay many of the fears which may accompany the idea of showing work to other members of the group, but the agreement to share the experience in this way must be made before the demand is made.

Certain ground rules need to be established before a 'showing' takes place: there must be absolute attention during the presentation; the purpose of showing must be clearly established and must include a desire to deepen the work and learn from the experience; the showing should always take place in the same space in which the work has been prepared and no real attempt at 'staging' should be involved. The individuals or group showing their work should decide where they want their audience to be but, generally speaking, they should simply gather round informally.

Questions or comments from the onlookers should be encouraged but, again, certain rules established. I was particularly impressed by a teacher I saw at work who insisted that the only permissible questions were what he called 'OK questions.' These were only to be positive so, for example, members of the group were permitted to ask, "Why are you doing this?" only if it did not imply "Why were you NOT doing that?"

The leader will, of course, set the tone for comment and discussion and will normally wish to ensure that encouragement is a major goal. The more supportive and accepting the tone of the session, the easier it is for comment and discussion to serve a genuine learning purpose.

The following suggestions envisage a situation where a number of individuals in the group are given orally or, better still, in written form, a situation or starting point from which they must evolve a scene with, if possible, a suitable resolution or ending. The time given for preparation will vary and will range from the almost spontaneous, where the improvisation unfolds in an extemporaneous fashion, to the more prepared piece. The entire activity is actually a variation on some of the oldest of party games and has re-emerged to great popularity as 'theatre sports' or improvised television games.

Suitable situations for improvisation are frequently amusing because there is a great deal to be said for introducing humour to counter-act embarrassment. A group laughing together, *with* each other rather than *at* each other, is often a very sensitive and supportive group. Nevertheless, there may be times when persuasion and tact may be necessary to create an entire group of willing participants. Such patience is often richly repaid by the growing sense of confidence and control that derives from some kind of public presentation.   .

Here are some possible starting points:

1) You are a musician carrying a cello. You hail a taxi, but getting into the taxi with your instrument proves more difficult than you anticipated.

2) You have to clean the windows on the eighth floor of a tall building.

3) A stray dog often comes into your garden, you decide to tie a label to its collar asking its owner to keep better control of the animal.

4) Locked out!

5) You are going to an important function and find that there is a problem with your clothes.

6) Wrongly accused of shoplifting in a supermarket.

7) You enter a crowded compartment in a train carrying a cat, a large bouquet and a heavy suitcase.

8) Driving a car you: cause a traffic jam by breaking down; hit a gatepost as you are turning into a drive; run into the back of another car.

9) A star mobbed by fans.

10) You are the soloist at a concert, but you find yourself wanting to sneeze.

11) An antique dealer in his shop suddenly smells burning.

12) You are the starter at an athletics meeting, but your gun wont fire, you make several attempts to start a race, but fail.

13) Caught riding a motorbike or bicycle the wrong way down a one-way street, or some other offence.

14) A shop assistant trying to please a difficult customer.

15) You are trying to conceal something: a split in your trousers; wearing odd socks; attending an interview wearing slippers; wrapping someone's present and he/she enters the room; Pip in *Great Expectations* smuggling a pie.

16) Attempting to eat spaghetti in a high-class restaurant; your friends have treated you to a meal that you find revolting.

17) Making a difficult delivery at a large house.

18) A baby-sitter cannot stop a baby crying.

19) Enter your hotel room to find something shocking.

20) You are left bound and gagged.

21) You arrive home to water pouring down the stairs.

22) Crossing a field with barbed-wire fencing and a bull.

23) You are trying to hang a huge, gilt-framed picture.

24) Crossing a very busy road to talk to an old friend.

25) You discover a strange object washed up on the beach.

26) An archaeologist makes an astounding discovery.

27) Cowboy coaxes a cow from a cattle truck into a pen.

28) You are sitting on a bench when . . . ?

29) Coming home to find a huge hole in your front garden.

30) An intruder enters your house.

31) Feeding pigeons in a city centre.

32) Bargain hunting in a crowded January Sale; visiting a car boot sale.

33) In the cinema you drop something valuable as you pull out a handkerchief.

34) Attempting to smuggle something through Customs.

35) Visiting strange people in hospital.

36) You are the only witness to a road accident.

37) A persistent salesperson comes to your door.

38) An unidentified flying object lands in your back garden, it may be difficult to convince others of the fact.

39) You are touring abroad when you are suddenly arrested, but you don't know why.

40) A doctor has a troublesome patient.

41) You are making your first call as a door-to-door salesperson or as a tele-sales person.

42) You are phoned, telling you that you have won a prize.

43) Trouble with your computer.

44) Understanding a form of transport abroad.

45) You are late for check-in at an airport.

46) Trying to conceal something you have broken.

47) Trying to rescue someone who has fallen into water.

48) Doing something noisy in a place where absolute silence is required.

49) Changing a light bulb in a difficult situation.

50) Your cat has climbed a tree and is stuck.

3

Working In Groups

Partnering

Drama is essentially a communal activity and provides real opportunities for co-operation and social development. Improvised drama is also an educational tool for the encouragement of inter-personal communication and the loss of inhibition.

A great deal of interesting work can be achieved in pairs: I always begin a session in which pairs are to be used by asking the group to work with the nearest person to them in the room at that moment and for the partners to call themselves A and B. There are probably more books with ideas for partnering work in drama than any other kind of drama source, so I shall confine my suggestions here to a few different kinds of activity of which it is possible to find many more examples.

The first feature of working with a partner is, obviously, to establish a level of trust. There are hundreds of so-called 'trust exercises' which are often used in various drama workshops and for classes in acting but they are equally widely used in other group situations such as therapy or rôle-play sessions. The idea is to enable each member of the pair to trust the other sufficiently to assist in physical tasks and to take responsibility for the other's safety and well-being. The ideas in this section are drawn from a number of varying traditions but will work well as extensions of the central idea of building trust, inventiveness and communal sensitivity.

(A) A Trust Exercise From T'ai Chi.

Partner A stands with his eyes closed. One of his or her hands is held out at approximately waist level with the palm facing down. *Partner B* supports this hand by his or her wrist, then *A* presses lightly down to ensure a sense of connection. *B* now moves slowly anywhere in the room and on whatever plane seems comfortable. *A* must keep his eyes closed but remain firmly attached to *B* by light pressure. *B* gradually makes the movements more complex and particularly changes levels as well as moving laterally. *A* will feel a floating sensation and a sense of helplessness. The partners then reverse.

(B) A Partner Game From Mime (pantomime in the USA.).

Partner A uses flat hands and sharply angled and bent hands to create an imaginary box as *Partner B* watches. Hands establish the exact size and shape of the box and *A* also conveys a sense of the weight of the box. It can be of any size, ranging from tiny to huge. *A* then passes the box to *B* who then places it gently on the floor and then creates another box which is eventually passed to *A*. The process is repeated many times. Then *A* creates a box large enough to contain *B* who then climbs into the box and *A* closes the lid. *A* then moves the box with *B* in it across the room. The whole process is then reversed.

(C) The Mirror Exercise Revisited.

I doubt if there is a drama teacher or facilitator living who has not, at some time, used the mirror exercise as a means of encouraging focus and co-operation. *A* and *B* face each other and take it in turns to lead or be the reflected image of the other's actions. In order to deepen the level of concentration the partners should work towards a state in which it is almost impossible to discern who is leading and who is following.

Particular attention should be drawn to the movement of the face, which often lags behind the flexibility and inventiveness of other parts of the body. Again, a sense of floating weightlessness will gradually take over as the concentration increases. Once that sense has been established, the pair can move on to the 'puppet and operator' activity.

Facing each other, the pair agree as to who is the puppet and who is the operator. The operator slowly lifts an arm and tells the puppet that there is a string attached to a particular limb or other part of the body such as the neck or shoulder. Initially the pair practice responding and leading. If A is the operator then B must be totally relaxed and try to isolate only that part of the body to which the imaginary string is attached. Eventually the operator will be able to make the puppet dance and then slowly sink to the floor in an inanimate heap as the strings are slackened. Some pairs might find it advantageous for the operator to stand on a chair behind the puppet and encourage the puppet to swing limbs freely before entering into more complex movements.

(D) Joint Stories.

In this activity, A and B take turns to invent and act out a spontaneous story. A and B tell one line or incident of the story each alternately and BOTH have to act out the events as they occur. There can be no pauses for thought or any other kind of hesitation, so pairs may prefer to have done a similar exercise in which they simply tell a story to each other before they attempt the simultaneous acting and telling version.

(E) A Basic Script.

The leader tells the group that there is a 'script' for A and B. The words are spoken to the group without expression or comment, except the instruction that they are to be memorised and that a short play is to be devised by two characters: *A* and *B* using ONLY these lines:

A: Are you getting through?
B: I think so.
A: Look out.
B: Ah!

(F) Under And Over The Chairs.

The group is divided into *A*s and *B*s. Sufficient chairs (the simpler in construction the better) are scattered around the room for all the *A*s to be seated. At a given signal all the *A*s begin to move over the chairs: they can stand on them, crawl over them, sit on them, or find any other way of remaining on the chairs. Simultaneously, the *B*s begin to move under the chairs: crawling on stomachs, sliding on backs or using whatever means of moving they can devise. After this has gone on for a few moments, another signal is given and at this point the group may only continue moving until there is someone ON and someone UNDER each chair. The *A*s look down at the *B*s and begin a conversation but the *B*s have to respond by creating an imaginary situation in which the two characters find themselves in this position. The pair then have to act out the complete story.

Group Work

For a group to work well together the members must have established sufficient trust and a sense of mutual purpose for genuine interaction to take place. It is difficult to give a precise point at which group work becomes feasible: many young children remain egocentric well beyond the early years of schooling and, rather like Bottom in *A Midsummer Night's Dream*, want to play all the 'best' parts. We all know, however, that similar behavioural characteristics may well persist well beyond childhood and that the decision to embark on group work remains a matter of judgement and sensitivity on the part of the group leader who should never be unduly discouraged if the work appears to fail.

Groups of about six or seven are probably the most workable and realistic. It is often better to select the groups so that a mix of abilities, sexes or personalities is achieved and there is no question of someone being obviously excluded. Groups often work best if they have a designated part of the room to which they frequently return and this can sometimes overcome the dispiriting situation of having no purpose-built or equipped drama space.

Once the task is set, preferably after considerable initial discussion, the leader has a delicate rôle: sometimes intervening to move a group onwards, sometimes giving the groups great freedom to work by themselves yet remaining in control of the process by determining the amount of time available or negotiating new agendas with the groups.

Sometimes, I suspect, the students' perception of the leader's rôle is one of some remoteness. Some years ago, I took a group of students to see some performances of short new plays in a 'fringe' theatre. On the whole, they were unimpressed by these plays and were rather restless (the sort of situation a teacher dreads!) but then there was a short play which showed three teenage girls who had been set an "Improvisation" by their drama teacher and were desperately trying to evolve something that would satisfy their teacher upon her imminent return, but at the same time indulge in all kinds of chat and interaction which seemed of infinitely more importance to them. At this point my students became absolutely wrapped in attention as if this was quite a familiar situation for them! I promptly decided to review my strategy for group work and found myself far less willing to say "I'll be back in five minutes to see what you have done."

(A) Give and Take: A Preliminary Activity.

Groups are formed and asked to make a working space somewhere in the room. One member of the group is asked to begin the activity; they simply have to begin moving in some way within the group space. After a while, a second member of the group must begin moving. At this point, the first person who was moving must freeze. A third person begins to move and the second person also freezes. This continues until all the group has moved. Then anyone in the group can move at any time, but there must only ever be one person moving at any one time. The rest must freeze. So each group member learns to take the floor and give it up by the most careful observation and group sensitivity. These factors must remain constant throughout all group work.

(B) Slave Driver.

Groups enjoy evolving scenes from a single title. A group of senior students had the theme 'Slave Driver'. They were working in the school library and the only equipment available included some steps, chairs and tables. The result of ten minutes preparation was as follows.

The slaves are rowing a galley driven on mercilessly by a man with a whip and a drum beat. One of the slaves slumps exhausted across his oar and the slave driver falls upon him to whip him into action. The other slaves manage to knock the slave driver and his assistant down and grab the key to unlock their chains. They then force the two task-masters to row the boat, whilst they enjoy their new-found liberty by sprawling in the sun and drinking.

All goes well until the ship approaches some rocks, whereupon they are seized by panic as their efforts to steer fail. When all seems lost they remember the two slave masters and, quickly freeing them, the slaves re-take their places at the oars and willingly submit to the lashes of the whip as they are steered to safety.

This scene, apart from having an interesting shape and well-defined climaxes, contained the element of conflict that usually makes the best drama; coupled with a nice sense of irony it also had the hint of social comment.

It utilised cramped conditions well and needed few props, and yet it provided a group of young people, some of whom would rarely read or watch a play, with an opportunity to think in dramatic terms.

Now try:

Apes; Arrest; The Ascent; Assassination; Caught!; Disaster; Escape; Execution; Exhibition; Expedition; Experiment; Fear; Feast; The First Night; Forgiven; Garrison; Haunted Panic; Heaven; Hell; Heresy; Highwayman; A Hit; The Hypnotist; Industrial Strife; Inquisition; Interrogation; Invention; Jealousy; The Moon; Nightmare; The Nineteenth Century; Ordeal; Outcast; The Pit; Plague; Pot Hole; Rebellion; Revolution; Siege; Smugglers; SOS; Temptation; The Trenches; Tunnel; Witch-hunt; Zoo.

(C) Adrift.

By the time that students have reached the stage in group work demanding climax and psychological perception, their leader might consider introducing plays which demonstrate how various playwrights have tackled similar situations.

The type of improvised scene dealt with in this section is particularly suitable as an example of the link between student and playwright but the ideas apply equally to most other categories. The tensions and stresses which build up when people are brought together in a confined space or when they are waiting are obvious.

After working on improvised scenes on the themes suggested below, the group can then explore: *Waiting for Godot* by Samuel Beckett; *The Cage Birds* by David Campton; *The Gioconda Smile* by Aldous Huxley; *In the Zone* by Eugene O'Neil; *The Dumb Waiter* by Harold Pinter; and *In Camera* and *Men Without Shadows* by Jean Paul Sartre.

A group of five students were asked to "Make a short scene about a number of people adrift in some sort of boat." Their scene showed a group of survivors paddling a rubber dinghy (represented by a ring of chairs). Various disputes arose until one man annoyed the others so much that, by various signals behind his back, they managed to throw him overboard. In different ways two others were disposed of (mainly on the grounds that survival is more likely for a small number). Two survivors remained. One of them attempted to knife the other, but in the process punctured the inflatable craft!

Now try:
A scene in which a balloon is launched but starts to sink and the passengers decide that one must jump out to save the others; trapped in a lift or a cable car; a train is buried in the snow; in a prison cell awaiting interrogation (perhaps based on George Orwell's *1984*); trapped in a mine or submarine; an underground train in the rush-hour; a waiting-room; a stage-coach and a hold-up; a family waiting for someone to arrive, or for news; a boxer is waiting to enter the ring, or any similar situation in a theatre dressing-room, etc; a coffee bar; a dispute breaks out at an auction; a mutiny; on an expedition one group member becomes seriously ill or is injured.

(D) The Isolate.

The problems of the outcasts of society make suitable discussion material to precede improvisation. The class can examine the various reasons, such as race, creed, conscience, unpleasant character or virtue, which lead to a person's being ostracised by a human group.

This scheme may be initiated by imagining a gang who make an outcast of one member for some reason and can then be extended to deal with universal problems. Students will be able to draw upon their experience and reading. They may, for instance, be able to comment on the attitude towards Simon in *The Lord of the Flies*, or towards Jews in European history or in Shakespeare's *The Merchant of Venice*.

After thinking about the problems of outcasts, a group of a dozen girls evolved a play called *The Isolate*. It showed how a schoolgirl, known to cheat in exams, was gradually driven into isolation by her contemporaries until she retreats into a dream world in which she imagines herself a teacher able to wield terrible power over other girls. This moving series of scenes was eventually scripted and staged with effective lighting in a Drama Festival.

Some of the following ideas are, of course, light-hearted and should prove amusing, but they have the essential ingredient of conflict. Try:

A reading room of a library - a mother enters with noisy children, or someone reads aloud or laughs at what he is reading (see Alan Ayckbourn's *Ernie's Incredible Illucinations*); a situation in which someone is wearing the wrong clothes; a crowd or group of spectators where one person makes ignorant and inappropriate comments; someone is excluded from a gang or group until he or she has gained acceptance by showing themselves to be as daring as the rest; an individual is ostracized because of a cultural difference, but eventually wins respect or suffers tragic consequences.

Other scenarios could be:

One person cannot speak the language of the others; farm animals laugh at a little puppy but soon discover his intelligence as a dog; Noah is mocked for building the Ark (see the *Medieval Mystery Plays*); a genius is mocked for a theory or invention - what are the results? - Copernicus and Galileo make astounding claims about the universe; an important or popular person is discovered to have leprosy (e.g. Naaman in the *Bible*, II Kings, Chapter 5) or another disease that involves prejudice; a teenager from an unco-operative family wants to achieve academic distinction; trying to find lodgings in an area of racial prejudice; gypsies attempt to set up camp in a beauty spot.

(E) Improvising Objects.

Students will have already had the opportunity of imagining themselves as objects as well as characters. The value of this work lies in freeing the body and its encouragement to those who find the subtler approaches needed for characterisation difficult. Careful planning and a due feeling for accuracy are also developed.

The following ideas can be broached by likening the desired effect to an animated cartoon in which everyday objects take on personality. Some of my students used a kitchen for a basis - one student was working there and went round the kitchen using various objects portrayed by the other students: taps, vacuum cleaner, saucepans, washing machine, dryer, refrigerator, microwave. Sound effects are also important.

Now try:
An invention of complex machinery - each person acting as a cog in a machine; clock mechanism, perhaps with moving figures; garage with petrol pumps, high pressure air pipe, etc; steam or beam engine - with perhaps the boiler bursting; computer or computer game; pistons of a car engine; amusement arcade; public house with beer pumps, cash register, fruit machine, swing door, swinging inn sign; railway station; carpenter's shop; factory; robots controlled by one person; erecting a tent on a windy day; loading a container ship or truck; fairground.

(F) Stills.

Still pictures, in which a group makes a frozen image like photography, can often capture the whole essence of an idea or scene. A few chairs or staging blocks can greatly increase the range of pictures that can be created. It is sometimes a good idea for one person to stand outside the group to help arrange them into a picture and it is possible to devise a complete story based on linked pictures. This suggestion is taken further in the section entitled **Family Album** in my chapter on therapy groups and can also make a good introduction to David Campton's play *Smile*, which is based entirely on the work of a photographer attempting to take a family portrait.

Initially, groups can work from a single title for their picture. This title can either be supplied or, at a later stage, provided by the group in response to something they have created. As an exercise this can also provide valuable preparation for work in production and the dynamics of blocking and grouping can be explored.

Here are some suggestions for possible group 'stills':
The Albert Memorial; An Egyptian Painting; Building a Pyramid; A Roman Meal; Coronation; The Guillotine; Nelson's Column; Hercules; Queen Elizabeth I Arrives; Imperial War Memorial; The Tomb; Showtime; Pancake Race; The Circus; Landing the Catch or Fishing; Fashion Show; The Team; Test of Strength; Fitness Centre or Gymnasium; The Proposal or The Christening; The Assembly Line; Picnic; Tug of War.

(G) Air.

The single titles in *Section A* give an opportunity for imaginative work in many directions. A more demanding form of improvisation emanates from the vague and sometimes abstract titles listed here. With an able group the demands made are equalled by the inventiveness displayed if preparation has been adequate. For example, a group of senior students had the title 'Air'. Their response has already formed the basis for a suggestion in *Section B*. A small circle of inward-facing chairs represented a balloon basket in which five people of various nationalities were floating in the sky. From the conversation it became obvious that, in spite of strenuous efforts, the balloon was sinking. One of the men, a desperate fellow who had only come on the adventure because his life had lost purpose, volunteered to jump into the abyss below to lighten the balloon; and this he did.

Still the balloon lost height and two more people jumped to their death, one for national glory, shouting "Vive la France!", and the other to satisfy conscience. With two passengers remaining, the balloon continued to sink and as they were sure that one could reach safety they decided to toss a silver coin to see which one would jump. One person spun a coin but to his horror the coin fell away from his grasp and he unthinkingly and perhaps symbolically precipitated himself over the side in a vain attempt to retrieve the coin.

Strangely enough, this group had not worked with the group who produced the inflatable dinghy scene described in *Section B.*

Now try:

Anticipation; Breath; Creation; Darkness; Death; Fire; Heat; Height; Joy; Justice; Life; Light; Luxury; Sorrow; Speed; Spring; Strength; Torture; Water; Weight.

(H) The Bible.

Perhaps no single source is so rich in suitable material for drama as *The Bible*. The three main reasons for this are:

1) that British drama has its roots in *The Bible* and Liturgy, and it is possible that at some stage teachers will want to link work with the intriguing early plays.

2) Biblical narrative is characterised by a nice economy of words that reduces stories to interesting essentials and leaves room for a great deal of imaginative work. Who can fail to be stimulated by the brief "In that night was Belshazzar the King slain"?

3) The stories, like drama, are concerned with the basic problems of our existence.

I was strongly criticised for the inclusion of this section in the first edition of this book. "What about life itself as a source?" asked the reviewer. Yet, since that time, the National Theatre's production of *The Mysteries*, entirely based on biblical stories and my own massive productions of similar plays in city centres in Britain have proved to be among the most popular of theatrical events because of their down-to-earth consideration of the human condition. Rock musicals and television dramas alike have taken their inspiration from biblical themes and Bertolt Brechts's *Parables for the Theatre* have demonstrated the potency of one powerful biblical form.

Teachers and leaders now have a bewildering range of new translations and adaptations of *The Bible* all claiming more accessibility or relevance. There is certainly no need to wrestle with the undoubted beauty but obscurity of the *Author-*

ised Version. Drama can, of course, be a means whereby the world's best-selling book is explored in a dynamic and imaginative way and there need be no question of an evangelical aim to the process. The same remarks might also apply to John Bunyan's *The Pilgrim's Progress,* the other great devotional book which we might associate with the values of the Victorian Sunday School, but which also contains rich metaphors and images which attempt to make sense of our existence.

There are several methods of using biblical themes. The story can be reproduced more or less accurately, although it will sometimes be necessary to alter parts of the story to fit the number of people available. It is frequently advisable to increase the size of groups to ten or twelve for this work: the stories of Elijah on Mount Carmel (using some of Mendelssohn's *Elijah*) or Belshazzar's Feast (with Sir Thomas Walton's music) given to such a group can produce exciting results. The teacher should always read the original story to the group first, so that they can enjoy the language and narrative style.

A second method is to modernise the stories. The parables are obvious examples, but older students will show real interest in improvised plays on the story of Jonah (see *It Should Happen To a Dog* by Wolf Mankovitz), or Noah in a modern, equivalent situation.

Thirdly, the stories can be used as a theme on which an entirely new play can be built. "The Garden of Eden", for instance, can produce Eve as a modern housewife and the serpent as a persuasive door-to-door salesman.

Now try: The Temptation - *Genesis* 3; Cain and Abel - *Genesis* 4; Noah - *Genesis* 6-9; Abraham and Isaac - *Genesis* 22; Esau and Jacob - *Genesis* 27; Joseph - *Genesis* 37-45; The Plagues and Exodus - *Exodus* 2, v. II - end of Chapter 1; Gideon - *Judges* 6-7; Elijah - *I Kings* 18; The Fiery Furnace - *Daniel* 3 and 5; David - *I & II Samuel*; Jonah - *Jonah*; Parables: Wheat and Tares - *Matthew* 13, 24-30; Talents - *Matthew* 25, 14-30; Wicked Husbandman - *Mark* 12, -9; Good Samaritan - *Luke* 10, 30-36; Prodigal Son - *Luke* 15, 11-32.

I suspect that the improvised Nativity Play will remain the most widely used form of school drama whatever our broader aims!

(I) The Problem of Violence.

Teachers who have worked with Primary, Middle or younger Secondary School children will know how frequently play-making involves brawling and fighting; and teachers of adolescents will testify to the reluctance with which their students move, unless provided with powerful motivation which often has violent roots. These two facts alone, make the controlled and organised fight a valuable part of a lesson.

The number of fights in literature is considerable and experience in arranging them not only gives an opportunity for studying stage violence, but gives insight into how the impact of a scene can be heightened. Few students realise, for instance, how the lines of Macbeth's fight with Macduff work as a dialogue until they understand the ponderous rhythm of an encounter with Scottish broadswords.

Stage falls should be taught to the whole group by the three stages of: kneel, sit, lie. Then, in pairs, the students can pretend to throttle each other, this being the simplest in slow motion. Gradually, as the group becomes more efficient, the final death or vanquishing of one of the combatants can be prolonged and then the complete fight made longer and choreographed. After this initial groundwork the fight can be incorporated into improvised scenes or the important link with a text forged.

Have a go at:
Wrestling on an imaginary cliff edge; fights and killings in pairs using the following imaginary weapons: battle-axes, broadswords, swords, mace and daggers as in medieval tournaments, rapiers, sword and shield, short sword versus trident and net, ancient and 'Western' pistols, knives.

Now stage various types of duel and work this in with a story or improvised scene. The important principle to establish is that the apparent receiver of a violent act, such as a punch or grip, has to do the majority of the work to create the illusion. Use the whole group to stage a battle, and accompany it with music, e.g. the final chords of *Mars* by Holst. Attempt fights with appropriate scenes from: *Macbeth, Hamlet, A Midsummer Night's Dream, The Caretaker, Julius Caesar, The Lord of the Flies, Murder in the Cathedral, View from the Bridge,* and *West Side Story.* Use ideas from slow motion T'ai Chi and other martial arts to add control and focus.

See *Great Fights in Literature* (published by Dent), *The Sword in the Stone* (T.H. White), *Ivanhoe* (Scott), and Homer's *The Iliad,* etc., for suitable material.

(J) The Tempest.

The improvised storm scene will provide plenty of opportunities for intelligent movement, sustained characterisation, lively dialogue and inventive use of props.

The first task of the students should be to convey the type of ship and then create the tension of the situation. Subjects can be treated almost entirely as dance drama with movement representing waves and swaying masts and rigging. In any case, music will prove helpful and the group can make excellent use of sound effects.

By superimposing selected lines from Scene I of *The Tempest* on to an improvised scene and gradually working towards the complete text, a far more vigorous and sincerely felt production can be achieved than if a group is confronted with the text and expected to produce action from it. For example, a group of middle school students devised a storm at sea. They showed the saloon of a luxury liner and the gradual change from ordered serenity to utter confusion as a storm arose. The movement of the ship was mirrored in the swaying of the crew and passengers, and when a man fell overboard he drifted out of reach by cunningly sliding along the floor while apparently trying to regain the ship. It is problems like this that give rise to enormous creativity.

Now set these tasks, perhaps by showing appropriate pictures or reading a story or report: A storm aboard a galleon, submarine, yacht or dinghy, cargo boat, airship, lifeboat, power boat or windsurfer.

Take *The Rime of the Ancient Mariner* and select suitable music to create some scenes.

(K) Sport.

Sport, of course, is a form of ritual and play and can provide an admirable basis for drama. For 'warming up' in a session, have pairs showing various sports in action, then go quickly round the room focusing attention on one pair at a time. Use: rowing, tennis, wrestling, fencing, volley ball, squash, boxing, cricket, soccer etc. Or create groups and give them the following details, preferably on paper:

1) On the village green in the early nineteenth century a cricket match is taking place. The players wear top hats and the bowling is underarm. Show the progress of three overs during the last of which the bowler attempts to bowl over-arm and a serious row ensues.

2) Ladies are playing tennis in their crinolines and, in an attempt to gain greater freedom, hitch up their skirts, revealing their ankles. Young gentlemen and a strict mother arrive.

3) A traditional tug-of-war takes place between rival teams stationed on opposite river banks - show what happens.

4) A weight-lifting championship.

5) A match starts - one side scores and a dispute arises.

6) Watching Wimbledon.

(L) Advertisements.

To some extent, drama can develop critical thinking. The insidious power of advertising is something which students can explore and recognise through improvisation and may, in fact, provide the basis of some in-depth work. All kinds of promotional material can be used as a starting point, but the production of imaginary television commercials is particularly valuable and enjoyable.

Approach this exercise from the following angles:
1) Create a commercial for a detergent, deodorant, drink, margarine, a breakfast cereal, a hair conditioner or shampoo, a night drink, eggs.
2) Show how you wish commercials known to you could end, for example, a dog in a dog food advertisement rolls over with stomach pains, or interviews in the street produce the wrong answers.
3) Create images you recognise as deliberately macho or sexist in appeal and discuss their underlying attitudes.

(M) Interviews.

Interviews not only give rise to creative work but have the entirely practical use of giving students an opportunity to examine appropriate strategies in an interview situation. They can range from the commonplace to the unusual. Of course, the formal interview is only one of many methods that are now used for making appointments. Others include games, rôle-playing, simulations and group encounters, all of which may well have potential for improvised drama and, indeed, have probably initially been devised by leaders and facilitators with drama skills.

An introductory group activity might work as follows:
1) Form groups of about six and give each member a number.
2) Tell all the students that they will be given a task which will involve some sort of leadership on their part and that they are to sustain the activity until the next person in the group takes over the leading rôle. The groups will work simultaneously and will need a fair amount of space. Ignorance of the skill that you may ask for the students to demonstrate is not acceptable as an excuse for not being fully involved!

3) All the activities are to be as spontaneous as possible and all the groups must react in accordance with the situation you have set up.
4) Begin with ALL the Number Ones.
5) Go round the group allocating their rôles in turn:

No. 1: You are a teacher of floral art and you have a new group of students gathered around you. Establish a way of working with them and try to impart the sense of harmony and peace that the Japanese associate with flower arranging.

No. 2: You have advertised in a local newspaper for people who wish to make good money selling a new product on a commission basis. Inspire the group who have responded to your advertisement and show how they go about selling. Make them go through some simulated sales situations.

No. 3: You are the director of a modelling agency and have recruited some new models for a mail order catalogue of fashion clothing. Give the new recruits their first lesson.

No. 4: You are the officer in charge of some new army recruits and you have to teach them some basic drill.

No. 5: You are leading a group in exploring the possibilities of meditation.

No. 6: You have to teach a short dance routine to a group of inexperienced amateurs for a local show.

No. 7: You are auditioning people for a new play in which you are seeking someone who can imitate a famous person.

No. 8: You are recruiting for a government agency and you tell the candidates the following scenario: A high-powered, overseas delegation has been visiting your country and you know that there is a real chance they will recommend awarding a major contract to your country. However, just after they left, you received a phone call from the manager of the hotel where they have been staying, saying that not only are all the bathrobes and towels gone but also the gold taps from the bathroom. How do you handle this situation?

Try the following scenarios:

An interview between an employer and prospective employee; colonel (or similar forces rank) interviews a recruit or someone applying for a commission; committee interview either a doctor who wants to be Medical Officer for their town or a prospective town planner; a housing committee hears the plea of homeless people, or considers requests for repairs and improvements; principal of a ballet school or the manager of a football team interviews a candidate; pop group try to persuade a record company to give them a recording test; barrister interviews a client in jail; door-to-door salesperson calls at the house; psychiatrist has a patient who says he is Henry VIII.

Link these with *Dock Brief* (John Mortimer), *The Winslow Boy* (Terrence Rattigan), *The Interview* (J.P. Donleavy), *Mr. Campion's Interview* (Brian Clark).

During interview activities the group can consider the rôle of body language and non-verbal communication and can experiment with strategies for putting others at ease, establishing authority or empathetic listening. It is often helpful to 'brief' the 'interviewers' as to their approach before introducing the 'candidate' into the situation.

(N) Mock Trial.

Court scenes might follow a visit to an Assize Court, but the constant interest in trial scenes on television and film leaves few people ignorant of the general procedure. The following account is of common practice in British Law; courts in the U.S.A. have slightly different procedures.

Select a **Judge**, who will preside over the trial and pronounce sentence in due course, a **Clerk of the Peace**, who reads the indictment and advises the **Judge** if called upon. There are usually two **Lawyers**. The **Prisoner** is in the dock guarded by two **Prison Warders**. There are the twelve members of the **Jury** and **Witnesses** for the prosecution and defence. The **Judge's Marshal** administers the oath to the jury and witnesses.

When the scene opens the public are in the gallery. The **Clerk of the Peace** arranges his papers and the **Lawyers** take their places. The **Jury** file into the jury box as their names are called out by the **Clerk of the Peace**, and everyone mentioned is ultimately seated. The **Judge** enters, preceded by the **Under Sheriff** and followed by the **Sheriff, Judge's Marshal** and **Chaplain**. The **Judge** carries a posy of herbs and wears white gloves. Everyone in Court rises. When the **Judge** is sitting, all others sit down.

On the first day of the trial, in the presence of the **Judge**, the **Jury** is presented to the **Prisoner** in case of objections to any one of them on personal grounds The members of the **Jury** are sworn in by the **Judge's Marshal**. Their oath is: *"You shall well and truly try and true deliverance make between our Sovereign Lady the Queen and the Prisoner at the Bar, whom you shall have in charge, and a true verdict give according to the evidence."* The **Jury** are sworn in in groups of four. Four Bibles and cards, on which the words of the oath have been printed, are used. Each member of the **Jury** holds the Testament in his or her right hand and nods in assent.

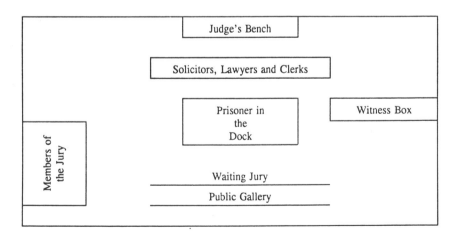

Figure 1: Arrangement for a mock trial in an English courtroom

DRAMA IMPROVISED

The **Clerk of the Peace** calls: *"Bring in the prisoner"* and then reads the indictment to the prisoner and takes the plea. If it is *"Not Guilty"* the case is tried in the following manner. The **Prosecuting Counsel** states the case and in due time calls **Witnesses**. The **Judge's Marshal** administers the oath to the **Witnesses**. Each **Witness** takes the Testament in the right hand and repeats the following: *"I swear (by Almighty God) that the evidence I shall give to the Court shall be the truth, the whole truth and nothing but the truth."*

Everyone listens carefully to the evidence, which is sometimes broken by the remarks of the **Judge**, who can put questions at any time and rule on points of law, and by the **Defending Counsel**, who can cross-examine the eye-witnesses for the prosecution. Then the **Defending Counsel** opens the defense case and calls **Witnesses**. They can be questioned by the **Judge** and cross-examined by **Prosecuting Counsel**. Finally, the **Judge** sums up the evidence, whilst the **Jury** listen and take notes. When the case is ended the **Jury** file out to consider their verdict and the **Judge** retires.

Before considering their verdict, the **Jury** elects a **Foreman** to chair their deliberations and present their verdict. When the **Jury** send word that they have reached their verdict, the **Prisoner** is brought back to the courtroom and the **Judge** returns. The charge is read again by the **Clerk of the Peace**.

The **Judge** says, *"Ladies and Gentlemen of the Jury, are you agreed upon your verdict?"* The **Foreman** answers, *"Yes, my Lord. We find the prisoner Guilty/Not Guilty."* If the verdict is guilty, the **Clerk of the Peace** tells the **Prisoner** to stand up to receive sentence. The **Judge** says: *"Have you anything to say or any reason why the Court should not pass sentence on you for the crime on which you are indicted?"* The **Judge** passes sentence, and the case ends.

In addition to straightforward trials attempt a:
Court in the French Revolution (see *A Tale of Two Cities*); trial of an historical figure - Charles I or for a humorous trial see *1066 And All That* by Sellar and Yeatman, published by Methuen or the dramatisation published by Samuel French; tribunal

hears evidence of war crimes and decides if "acting under orders" is admissible as a defense.

(O) Sound Work.

Improvisation can produce very imaginative work in sound only. For this activity two things are essential:
1) a means of concealing the performing group from view;
2) a clearly defined aim, such as a radio play beyond.
One other thing is highly desirable: some means of sound recording.

In the first stage, groups produce in sound only their impression of some suitable subject. It is remarkable what can be achieved by the voice and some percussive sounds, but it is advisable to have handy a box containing some props, such as tin mugs or coins. In no activity is it more important to have a pre-arranged signal for immediate cessation of noise and a thorough investigation as to what will be in progress in the adjoining rooms!

The groups take turns at going out of sight to make and, if possible, record their noises. When this stage has been passed, a plot suitable to the noises can be created and, eventually, a scripted radio or puppet play may be devised.

Try:

A railway station in the days of steam; building site; dockyard; launching an astronaut; underground train or tram; Emergency Services in action; windy night at sea or in an old inn; sports or national event commentary; sounds of rowing and a river; diver descending. Many of the stories already mentioned in this book are suitable.

(O) Music.

We have already seen that music often enhances a drama lesson. Indeed, the affinity of the subject with the study of music and movement (which is established as a child first gives dramatic quality to movements or responds to rhythm) should never be overlooked. The main difficulty in the use of music as a starting point for a group improvisation is the wide variety of response to so subjective a stimulus. Suitable music can often accompany a narrative or provide shape to an activity; it may also establish mood, tension or climax but, sometimes it is advisable to couple music with a more concrete idea. Situations which relate to the playing of musical instruments are suitable for brief scenes and exercises and give opportunity for characterisation.

Try:
A conductor enters as the orchestra tune up and they start to play; miming to a record of Britten's *Variations on a Theme of Purcell - The Young Person's Guide to the Orchestra*; country and western band; the band plays while people stroll in the park in Victorian times; jazz band in New Orleans; rock group sets up and plays.

What is the group's response to: Ravel's *Bolero*; *Post Horn Gallop*; *Death of Ase* or *Morning* from *Peer Gynt*; Widor's *Organ Toccata* from his *Fifth Symphony*; electronic or synthesised music or various 'New Age' tracks designed for meditation.

(P) The Map.

The following activity grew out of some time spent looking at maps and at some of the evocative names used to describe topographical features. For example, there is an area near the Rivers Medway and Thames marked on the map as "Bedlam's Bottom" which appears to accord with the area where Dickens set the opening moments of Pip's meeting with the convict in *Great Expectations*. And, on a recent visit to North West America, I was taken by a friend to see "Jump off Joe Lake". Such names are dense with history and can themselves form a source of drama.

At one time I devised a project with a group in which we linked all the events we could discover in connection with the River Thames and then, after the students had worked on this with considerable enthusiasm, we repeated the process in relation to a number of major roads. Again, we were constantly struck by the richness of names: their origins, their descriptiveness and some of their obscurities. Such things always have dramatic potential.

The particular activity I am about to describe builds on this potential and falls into a number of natural stages:

1) A number of groups are formed and each group has a large sheet of paper and a selection of marker pens and/or colored pencils. The groups each draw an outline map of an imaginary island and then each group member in turn adds to the map a topographical feature and gives it a name. This process is repeated until there are at least a dozen named and varying features on the map.

2) Each group decides on some treasure or hidden feature to which the map might be a clue and then, on the reverse side of the paper, gives a series of instructions as to how to find the treasure by following the map and encountering its features.

3) The maps are then collected and redistributed to other groups to study. They then each elect a leader who will become their expedition leader.

4) We imagine that the expedition leaders have acquired the maps and have advertised for potential members of an expedition. The group members are those who have responded to the advertisement and the first 'scene' is the initial meeting.

5) From this point, the drama may take many forms. It may involve a session in which individuals have to convince the leader of their fitness to go with them, or it may include a time in which each person speaks of the skills they bring with them. At some stage, however, the journey itself begins.

6) The groups create imaginary environments and act out the expedition, following closely the map and its instructions. Crises of all kinds may develop and extensive dramas may derive from the original starting point.

(Q) Rites and Rituals

Drama, as we understand it, almost certainly has its origins in ritual and dance. It is therefore not surprising that improvised drama, which is in some ways spontaneous, should be successful when based on rites and rituals: which are spontaneous reactions to beliefs. Drama of this kind must have a sense of timing, visual balance and symbolic movement and rhythm. Movement may be expansive or minute, violent or restrained, but always controlled.

Try a:
Religious ceremony in Early Britain at Stonehenge (Rosemary Sutcliffe, *The Eagle of the Ninth*); ritual in Ancient Greece (Jean Paul Sartre, *The Flies*); burial of a Pharaoh; ceremony in the land of the Aztecs (Peter Shaffer's *Royal Hunt of the Sun*).

We have previously seen how myths from various cultures have archetypal dramatic qualities. This is certainly true of Native American mythology, especially those myths associated with Creation and the coming of white people to North America. My own play, *Turtle Island*, developed from a series of improvisations based on a great speech by Chief Seattle in which he questioned the whole concept of land-ownership and drew attention to the disastrous environmental impact of European attitudes to the earth. Each point in his speech can be related to myths and legends which can be told ritually to an imaginary assembled tribe. Sections of another of my plays, *Beowulf*, can be treated in a similar way in an imaginary, Anglo-Saxon setting.

4

Working with Larger Groups

Small group improvisation is not always suitable because (1) the leader has to delegate freedom in such a way that some disorder may result; (2) the students are not old enough to co-operate in groups; (3) there is insufficient space. The solution may lie in using the whole group as one unit and acting a story. All the students should be aware of the story, as they all need to participate. An example of how this might work is as follows, however, the outline is by no means rigid.

The teacher selects the Norse myth of Balder and commits the story to memory, possibly also reading Arnold's poem *Balder Dead*. The story is told to the group and excerpts read from the poem. The story is then discussed and 'scenes' suggested and noted on a blackboard or flip chart. The leader reduces the suggestions to these:

1) Odin and Freya discuss their son, and decide to send their messenger to ask everything in the world to promise not to harm him; the messenger is summoned and sent.

2) The messenger goes in turn to as many elements and creatures as can be represented and they each promise.

3) The gods in Asgard throw spears and other missiles at Balder while Loki, jealous, decides to find a means of harming Balder.

4) He goes to the old woman at the end of the world, who eventually tells Loki of the mistletoe - he cuts a bough.

5) In Asgard the gods continue their sport. Hoder regrets that he can't participate - Loki inveigles him into throwing a shaft of mistletoe - Balder dies and Hoder kills himself.

6) The building of the pyre and the launching of the ship (usually the leader's desk).

7) Hermod's journey to Hela's realm.

8) He asks all things to weep - but the old woman laughs - he bids farewell to Balder.

At first, all the dialogue is improvised but may be polished later on. This play could occupy a group of forty by casting them thus: Balder, Odin, Hela, Messenger (Hermod), Bridgeman, Elements such as water and rock, Loki, Freya, Old Woman, Hoder, Thor and 10 gods, Animals - fifteen, Ghosts in Hela's realm - five. In a smaller group, the gods, ghosts and animals can be played by the same students.

The scenes are carried out under the direction of the leader who may have to supply a narration to give encouragement and shape. You can also use: *Pilgrim's Progress*; Bible stories like 'The Exodus'; the landing of the Martians from *War of the Worlds* (H. G. Wells); *Lord of the Flies*; *The Rime of the Ancient Mariner*; *The Pied Piper of Hamelin*; *Flannan Isle* (W. Gibson); *The Inferno* (Dante - John Ciardi's translation); blowing up the bridge from *For Whom the Bell Tolls* (Ernest Hemingway); or stories from *The Argonauts*, *The Iliad* or *Odyssey*.

Similar techniques can be used to turn documentary, historical or 'living newspaper' material into drama. In recent years, there have been exciting developments in play-making using entire communities. Such works, as undertaken by the *Living Archive Theatre Project* in Milton Keynes or by Ann Jellicoe in a number of British towns, have used improvisation to explore memories, photographs, press cuttings and other archival material and create community plays with huge numbers of participants.

5

Working with Therapy Groups

Throughout this book, I have tried to suggest that improvisation is an effective means of creating a situation in which genuine play takes place and also provides a way of understanding our complex lives. In the course of the work, emotions, motives, inhibitions, attitudes or sources of inner energy may all be explored; all of which have an obvious application to therapy. Many of the practical suggestions contained here are suitable as a basis for work in therapy, but I have selected three more extended examples to demonstrate some ways of working and some of the possibilities which might be considered.

This is by no means intended as an exhaustive thesis on dramatherapy, but it may not only serve the purpose of giving concrete ideas, but also of highlighting what seems to me to be the danger of dramatherapy: it is so often practised by those with extensive knowledge of and feeling for therapy but with little knowledge of or feeling for drama.

The following suggestions are offered in the form of three projects which have been successfully used in a variety of therapy situations.

Family Album

We work in small groups of about six members. If it is possible to mix the sexes equally that will be helpful but by no means essential. The leader introduces the idea of family portraits: perhaps those faded, yellowing photographs from long ago, but also the group photographs we still create.

Each group stages a family group pose after discussion as to the various ages and identities of the members. The groups also decide what event is taking place at the time of the photograph: is it a family celebration of some kind? Is it an outing or visit? The photograph is given a title so that when it is stuck in the family album, subsequent generations will know what is going on. The groups work at holding their positions for a while, so that all the photographs can be seen by everybody.

Each member of each group then decides on a brief sentence or two to speak which describes who they are, their age, their relationship to everyone else in the photograph. The photographs are formed again and each person speaks their sentence in a direct and non-emotional tone. The groups discuss content again and each member adds a further sentence or two describing how they are feeling at that moment and why.

Again the photographs are formed and the characters (as they have now become) speak their words. Each group then devises six more photographs to include in the family album. Each new image must have a title and may have taken place before or after the original picture. These new photographs need not include every member of the group in each picture. The sequence of photographs is then shown to and shared with the entire group and the leader guides a session of "OK questions" and discussion.

Suggestions are made as to which photograph(s) from each group could be developed into an extended scene with dialogue. The activity might begin with several photographs being brought to life before further discussion and rehearsal establishes the actions, reactions and sub-text of the scene. Groups which have established a high level of trust or 'closed' groups may move on to a more personal stage in this exercise. Each member of the groups creates a drama about themselves, by creating pictures of their own past and working through events and relationships by creating, not only a script based on the real events, but also demonstrating alternatives to what actually happened. The creator of the group play is supported by the rest of their group and the sharing with others is sensitively led by the facilitator.

The exercises may be a valuable coming to terms with the past and a liberating and healing experience. The sense of 'acting out' may also be of benefit to the participants as they help to give shape and meaning to other people's stories.

Abigail Is Leaving

This activity may work well in a single, large group or a series of smaller groups and there are a number of strategies for enabling the drama to take place. Abigail (this is the name chosen by the first group with whom I undertook this project) is an intelligent and talented person of eighteen or nineteen years of age. Everyone has high but conventional expectations of Abigail and what she will achieve. Everyone who knows her is stunned when she declares that she is abandoning the life she has led so far and the future that appears to be planned for, and by, her, in favour of some totally different alternative.

In discussion, the group begins to establish details of the story and when agreement has been reached on the context a group member is selected to be Abigail. All other members select a rôle for themselves of someone who, in some way, relates to Abigail. These might include parents, brothers and sisters, teachers, friends, relations, friends of parents, tutors, doctors, ministers of religion - whoever might have some impact on Abigail's life.

Abigail sits in the middle of a circle formed by the group members. Each character in turn makes a statement to Abigail. At the end, Abigail makes a statement about her predicament.

To help in the construction of the drama, it might be appropriate to utilise the four suggestions for initial play study that appear in my book *How to Study Modern Drama* (published by Macmillan):

1) Identify the protagonist's predicament.
2) Identify the world of the play and its social order.
3) Identify the tensions and threats.
4) Achieve a broad outline of the action.

Now hold a series of meetings: these take place between any number of characters but they all relate to the problems with Abigail. Once the order and nature of the meetings have been planned, these become 'scenes' in the play and may be acted out as spontaneously as possible. If it is possible to include some scenes involving a large number of characters this will give the total play a less rambling shape. Once the scenes have been acted out, they may be shown, polished or repeated in any way which helps the work to acquire depth.

The leader observes the work and selects an appropriate time to introduce the next phase. Each character has to write a speech which reflects aspects of their dilemma and inner-most thoughts. It will probably be equivalent to a long paragraph but will be punctuated by pauses, hesitations and other features of everyday speech. I have found it helpful to read an example of such a speech *before* the task is set, but I have been constantly amazed at the quality of writing that can be produced by asking people to take time and quietness to undertake this activity.

The speech may be a soliloquy or personal statement of the kind that is used so effectively in John Godber's play *Bouncers*. It may even be memorised by committed group members if the project spans a number of sessions. Once the speeches have been written, they should be shared with the rest of the group and some modifications may be made if suggestions are positive and supportive. The group then devises a means of inserting the speeches into the action of the scenes. One useful technique is to play the scenes and have the action freeze at certain points for one of the characters to speak their speech, but there are many other possibilities.

I recently worked with a group who wrote some of their speeches to be delivered by two characters almost simultaneously from two sides of the acting area. The characters spoke a few words or phrases alternately and at one point delivered a key line together. The irony of two characters both speaking the same words, but loaded with meaning from their own point of view, was extremely powerful.

To illustrate this futher, I shall give an account of a play on a similar topic, devised entirely through improvisation, by a group in North West America. The account is written by one of the group members:

A Journey

"First let us begin with the action of the play. The play reveals the story of a young girl who makes a decision to leave the home she has lived in since her birth. This is a quite momentous and gutsy decision which seems to relate to her strong minded character, yet she winds up changing her mind and never leaving the bus station.

The protagonist of the play is Jenny, an eighteen year old, who has just graduated from high school. Her predicament is this: she is uncertain that staying in her small town, getting married and living just as her parents and everyone else in the stagnant place has, is what she wants out of life. She feels she wants more, yet leaving is not an easy decision, to say the least. While many forces push her to leave (her parents, the thought of an unfulfilled life), others pull her to stay (her sister, the comfort of the known, safe environment she has lived in all her life). Then there is Earl, her boyfriend, who, interestingly enough, acts as both a force to push her away and keep her there. She loves him, yet is afraid that marrying him (which is what he wants) would doom her to the life she does not desire

The tensions and threats are mainly focused on Jenny. Her tension is with her parents and the town in general, with the unknown beyond the town, with leaving her sister and Earl behind. Yet there are other tensions and threats. One threat is the disruptive effect her leaving would have on the ones who care for her. Her parents also feel tension in that they want her to settle down and be secure, yet she seems somewhat resistant to the idea of doing what they say. Earl, who is nineteen, feels pressure to marry Jenny, as everyone expects him to do so. The threat here is that if Jenny leaves him, he may be shattered. Jenny leaving is the last thing he would ever consider happening, so it would have a remarkable effect upon the heretofore narrow-minded young man. Jenny's sister also faces the threat of facing the small town life without the support of her sister, and is torn between wanting her to stay and wanting her to go.

The social world of the play is that of a very small town, most likely one with a population of no more than a few hundred. In towns such as this, life is somewhat slow. One grows up to do what your father does, girls grow up to marry and have children who will do the same. Also, in small towns such as this, very conservative attitudes pervade the atmosphere; change and novelties are looked at with suspicion and mistrust. The stark smallness of the town affects the social order also, for the structure of the family and, indeed, of the town as a whole, is alarmingly patriarchal. Father and the church know best. Such that Jenny leaving and turning down a proposal from Earl would seem unheard of. Yet Jenny, although opposed to this, eventually stays."

Here is an example of a speech from the same play, together with an analysis by the writer and performer:

Jenny: Why did he do that? Why, all of a sudden, does everyone think that I should get married? Damn him! Everything was fine just the way it was. *(With wonder and some love shining through.)* He asked me to marry him. I had dreamed of this day *(now with some confusion)*, but I guess I didn't expect it to be so soon. I didn't expect it to be Earl. I had planned on saying yes.

But, when the actual words came out, I couldn't say it. I said no
. . . *(almost shouting)*. No! I can't say yes. I can't give everything
up; not yet, not before I've had a chance to live my life. *(Softly,*
regretfully.) I love him and I think I want to marry him, but I'm
just not ready yet. Getting married would mean never leaving,
never seeing anything new, just staying at home and having
babies and cooking . . . *(louder, more decisive)*. I don't need a
husband to survive and he sure as hell doesn't need a wife. He
still lives at home with his parents. *(Shouting and then slowly*
calming down and gaining control.) Dammit, Earl! Yes, I love you.
Yes, I want to marry you! No, I love you, but I will not be letting
you win this one. To hell with y'all! There is more to life than
grain prices and broken down tractors. I'm going to go see new
things. If you won't let me stay here and be myself, then fine,
I'll leave.

"**Jenny's** main speech sums up her dissatisfaction with
the status quo of small-town life. As a young person in a small,
traditional, agricultural area, she is expected to follow the
standard patterns of getting married young, having babies and
taking care of the farm. However, she is an intelligent, young
woman from a new generation. She wants to leave the small-
town life and develop a new way of life for herself. At nearly
every point in the play, she finds herself repelled by the status
quo and then drawn back by love and security.

This is really the only time **Jenny** has a chance to verbally
express all her feelings, without the interruption of her family
or **Earl**. This speech marks a turning point in the play. She
breaks away from her family and boyfriend; deciding to take
control over her own life. The speech really shows how she is
torn between the two directions her life may take. She can only
choose one, and that choice will determine the rest of her life.

The speech is interesting in itself. It is divided into two
parts, which are separated by the two pieces of **Earl's** main
speech. **Jenny's** speech is significantly different to **Earl's**; she
sounds more coherent and better educated and her speech
becomes more organised and calmer as it progresses. **Earl**

DRAMA IMPROVISED

sounds like an ill-educated hick from the sticks. In general, **Jenny** sounds more literate than the other characters. This reinforces the differences between herself and her environment. The first part of the speech is very disjointed and full of pauses, while she is thinking. A lot of conflicting emotions are portrayed in the first part. The second part shows **Jenny** calming down and taking control. There are less pauses, less emotion and her thoughts seem to travel more linearly.

    Jenny must decide to stay or leave. The speech signifies her working it out in her mind, with just a few pieces being vocalised. The speech isn't directed toward anyone, so the audience members are the only ones that hear her. The other characters do not hear her because she is making a decision and must do it herself, without outside interference. Most of the speech is made up of short segmental sentences and questions, separated by long pauses for thought. The questions seem to be directed to **Earl** or the audience, but are really only in **Jenny's** head, helping her to direct her thoughts toward a decision.

    The flow of **Jenny's** speech is quite disjointed. This is due to the pauses for thought. The verbal pieces that the audience hears are just little snippets that **Jenny** verbalises whilst thinking. A 'normal speech' would usually be smoother and more planned out than **Jenny's**, but she is just talking to herself. This forces the audience to see and feel more of what **Jenny** is thinking and feeling.

    I believe this is a very effective speech. It sums up the theme of the play, which is young people and new ideas trying to overcome older, more traditional ways. Because the speech is from inside **Jenny's** head, it gives the audience a good chance to really know where she's coming from. This is a major turning point in her life and the speech is where she decides the way the rest of her life will go."

A Forum in the Mode of Boal

    The great, South American, director, Augusto Boal, is the author of the inspirational books, *The Theatre of the Oppressed* and *Games for Actors and Non-Actors*. When Boal first came to

52

Europe, he was amazed to find that the oppression which most people felt was not of repressive political regimes or systems, but an oppression of the mind by forces which often seemed to originate from within. Instead of living in fear of "the cops", he reckoned that most of the individuals who attended his workshops lived in fear of what their subconscious was doing to them. Thus he invented the phrase "a cop in the head". The technique which Boal originally devised to activate communities in getting involved in their own destiny and political future he termed 'forum theatre', but he later adapted the system of working to include therapy groups. In forum theatre, a company of actors acts out a situation which members of the 'audience' have suggested.

The situation has to be of deep significance to the spectators and will, invariably, be to do with some issue which affects the life of the community in which the forum is taking place. The actors work hard to play the rôles assigned to them, making every effort to understand the relative positions of power which their character wields and what behavioural options are open to them. As situations are acted out, the action may, at any time, be interrupted by a spectator who may suggest different ways of handling the situation and other strategies for achieving goals by both individuals and groups.

My own first attempts to work in this way with a therapy group were very tentative, but I discovered that, in a supportive and 'safe' environment, there were a substantial number of group members willing to have their own lives used as subjects for a forum theatre piece; and others who were equally willing to take on rôles and to show a flexibility in being able to respond to the suggestions of the spectators which was quite astonishing. The activity has much in common with, and may serve as an extension of, the **Family Album** idea mentioned earlier in this chapter.

This is one possible way of working:

1) The participants work in small groups and there should be a warm, comfortable atmosphere. If possible, the room should be carpeted, with the provision of floor cushions or a supply of easy chairs.

2) The leader suggests that members of each group try to recall an event in their lives which had to do with problems of communication or conflicting wishes.

3) Members share their recollections with the other members of their group.

4) One of the events is selected initially by each group and the teller of the story organises a re-enactment of their event by casting other group members in the various rôles. The person whose story this is takes care to suggest the most accurate dialogue and action to capture both the essence and detail of the memory. The teller may elect to 'play themself' or have someone else do this.

5) Everyone in the room then comes together to watch the drama devised by the small groups. As the spectators watch, they may suggest how the situation might have been avoided or, perhaps, made less painful. If there is a particular sense of caring in the group, the spectators can invite the person whose story they are witnessing to go back to those events and say now what they might have said then or say to the characters of the drama what they feel they wish to say now.

Variations on the forum technique might involve acting out the story in a different way to provide an alternative ending. When questioned about why he had spent an entire life in the Arts a great teacher once said to me, "The Arts always provide an alternative way of looking at things." This seems to me to be a supreme justification for the Arts therapies.

Activities such as those outlined in this chapter require particular skill on the part of the leader. Issues may well arise which are painful, disturbing and challenging. One of my main concerns with some of the developments in Drama in Education, during the sixties and seventies especially, was that drama teachers and leaders of workshops were setting themselves up as High Priests or holders of Universal Knowledge encouraging their students and clients to reveal intimate and unexplored aspects of themselves, or to investigate complex areas of human relationships without actually having the training, skill or humility to handle, to use the therapy jargon, "the stuff which came up." Leaders should be aware of the potentially volatile and personal material with which they may be dealing and cultivate skills of good listening, sympathy and humility. And in anticipation of the cry of therapists saying "Is that *all* you need?", I add that the moment that the need for further training becomes obvious it must be sought.

6

Teachers and Scripts

Improvisation can be a means of both creating and approaching a script. Elements of script writing are contained within many of the activities we have examined and there are times when an engagement with an already written play can be illuminated through improvisation.

For teachers working in schools and colleges there is often a dilemma: their subject will only achieve high status if it is seen to culminate in a public production or if it involves the study of play texts. In either case this may run contrary to the aims of creative drama teaching and even negate the enthusiasm and imaginative quality of what may have been achieved through improvisation. A great number of attainments expected of our students are tied to literacy and there is the real danger that the drama lesson can end up as yet another source of failure.

The demand for public performance will derive from a total misunderstanding of the nature of much good drama teaching. Nevertheless, there are, and have been, excellent examples of plays created through improvisation which provide effective theatre. Plays which demand *public* improvisation are notoriously perilous and are best avoided altogether.

On the other hand, a piece which has originated in improvisation may be deepened and given a greater sense of form and structure if it is prepared for showing. In a similar way, elements of improvisation can be used to give a scripted play far greater dynamism and focus. It is remarkable how often improvisational techniques are abandoned in the pressured time of rehearsal, in favour of an almost dictatorial style when, in fact, a freer, more experimental approach will produce more meaningful results.

Improvisation is a tool, rarely an end in itself, and it may lead to a variety of outcomes. I have suggested at times in this book that an issue explored through an improvisation may be taken further by finding a play which deals with a similar topic. This is particularly helpful if the study of plays is required. But the idea of plays as simply another branch of literature is extremely limited. The whole process might, however, work in reverse if the teacher wants to introduce a script for performance by a group. After becoming thoroughly familiar with the script, the teacher might create some improvisations as preparatory work before using the script. This can often help avoid the static effect of having scripts in hands. As we have seen, improvisation can explore character, situation, motives, tensions and much of what Stanislavsky termed "the given circumstances" and can free students from the idea that a play is words with actions.

Through improvisation, students can investigate what it is that makes a character utter those words and do those things which the playwright has assigned them and what that character is also doing at times when it appears that the playwright has assigned them to do nothing. One of the school examinations in drama that has its roots in improvisation as a core activity nominates "the ability to adopt and sustain a rôle" as one of its major criteria for evaluation. It is precisely these qualities which are often lacking in performance when students use scripts. Through improvisation, the necessary exploratory work can be carried out.

Fortunately there has been a quiet revolution in the quality of scripts being published for use in an educational context during the last 25 years. Not only have the scripts themselves been attractively presented and made more accessible in format, but the topics have increasingly reflected students' experience of the real world and their need to relate to it. Even more encouraging has been the attention of major playwrights to the needs of teachers and group leaders and the willingness of publishers to consider scripts emanating from improvisation-based work in classrooms, studios and youth theatres.

Many of the new plays deal with serious issues and yet are sufficiently short to make their use as part of a teaching scheme realistic. Flexible casting and staging ideas also contribute to making collections of such plays valuable resources for drama teaching. The anxiety remains, however, that once a script is introduced, the level of participation of an entire teaching group may be difficult to sustain, and the efforts of leaders to maintain high levels of energy and imagination may have to be increased if the creativity they have worked so hard to achieve is not to be lost.

The appearance of plays specifically intended for the educational market by no means precludes the use of established classics of the modern or any other theatre. Again, improvisation can inform ways of adapting, shortening and presenting a whole range of material from almost every theatrical tradition and period. The act of theatre is never archaeology nor just breathing new life into old bones, it is the act of finding the significant and creating it afresh.

Such a degree of personal creativity makes enormous demands and the constant need to restock, rethink, recharge and reflect is the only real justification for this book and its reissue. I have continually suggested reference to many kinds of source material as a means of ensuring that, even with the absence of short courses and a network of advisers, there are means whereby ideas can continue to flow and expand.

7

Shakespeare Workshop

In the early years of this century, the remarkable Lilian Baylis established the "Old Vic" theatre in London as the centre of innovative productions of Shakespeare's plays and as the only theatre, at that time, where the entire Shakespeare canon was presented in rotation. Lilian Baylis had no particular experience of Shakespeare, but an unerring sense of theatre and its relevance to life and to the experiences of ordinary people. Almost every great English actor of the first three-quarters of this century owed something to the "Old Vic" and on one occasion, Lilian Baylis sent for the talented Sybil Thorndike to suggest that she might consider playing the part of Lady Macbeth. Sybil Thorndike, conscious of the great traditions of Lady Macbeths, showed some hesitation, but the forthright Miss Baylis had no time for such attitudes: "I don't know what all the fuss is about with these 'great parts'," she said, "they're all very easy. You've only got to *be* people. You know them all, well just BE them. I think Lady Macbeth is a very easy part for you. She loved her husband and wanted him to get to the top of the tree; I expect you feel that way too!"

Now, this apparently simplistic approach to Shakespeare may strike us as banal, but Lilian Baylis had both demythologised Shakespeare *and* cut through most of the absurd barriers we continue to erect around his plays. It is no coincidence that it was at the "Old Vic" schools' matinees that generations of teenagers had their first experience of live Shakespeare and that in their experience of performing in this situation, many actors developed initiatives for bringing drama into schools. Brian Way, who wrote one of the most influential books on drama teaching, dates his determination to find a way of retaining children's attention through an intimate theatre style from his experience of Shakespeare at the "Old Vic".

Sooner or later most drama teachers will confront Shakespeare, not only because of his secure place in the National Curriculum, but also because there seems to be no aspect of the human condition with which his plays **do not** deal superbly. In our time, Charles Marowitz has demonstrated that Shakespeare's texts can simply be a basis for further construction and improvisation. His book *Recycling Shakespeare*, documents many of the collages and re-workings which he has presided over, enraging some and delighting others in his attempt, once again, to debunk the solemn Shakespeare industry.

It is hardly new to suggest that Shakespeare is accessible and open to improvisation: the dramatist himself made use of 'dumb show', which is really an extended form of improvisation on the plot of the play and which, according to a speech in *Hamlet,* was a great favourite with the "groundlings". In some respects, given falling standards of literacy and familiarity with such language as the Authorised Version of *The Bible,* many of our students might as well be groundlings for all that they are able to bring to an understanding of a Shakespeare play! This may give us a starting point for the exploration of themes and issues in any Shakespeare play using our improvisation techniques. We will leave aside, for a moment, the difficult question of Shakespeare's language.

Here are some activities which have been designed to make a play more approachable:

1) Devise a 'dumb show' (a play in mime only, without dialogue) showing the entire plot of the play in outline. Allow a time limit of five minutes.

2) Take a scene between two or three characters from a Shakespeare play and have each speaker create an audible 'thought bubble' between each of their speeches.

3) Select a very minor character from the play and have him or her as the centre of an improvised scene: perhaps telling the story to another imaginary character.

4) Here are some of the issues with which Shakespeare's plays deal: Problems of Royalty; Tensions between Families and between Parents and Children; Violence and Gang Warfare; Living with a Conscience; The Use of Power and the Ideas of Justice and Injustice; Love, Sex and Relationships; War between Nations and Rival Groups; Ambition, Indecision and Ideas of Freedom; Nature, Magic and the Supernatural; The Problems of Old Age; Political Power and Intrigue; Ideas of Good and Evil; God and the Human Race.

Taking some of these subjects in relation to a particluar play, devise either a TV news item or radio report to explore the idea or create a scene in an imaginary press office where a 'story' is being hunted down and made into headline news.

5) Take a main character from a play and 'hot seat' them in groups. This means that any questions concerning their background, motives or reactions may be asked.

6) Select a short scene from the play and work on it in the way that Brecht sometimes did, i.e. characters speak in the third person, introducing each speech with words like, "She said sadly", or "Picking up the cup, he replied". Compare this with the extract from Brecht's *The Story Teller* on page 6 of this book and then replay the scene using a story teller.

Many teachers feel quite comfortable about devising such activities to find relevance and interest for their students and, inevitably, a great deal will depend on the ability and motivation of those students. However, it is the language of the plays which so often causes anxiety. I am, therefore, going to conclude with an extended example of the creative thinking and imaginative approach of one Theatre-in-Education company, who devised a programme for presentation to students in the early days of meeting with Shakespeare.

Like the Oregon Shakespeare Theatre in the United States of America, the Channel Theatre Company in Britain has survived the cuts of recent years, to take live theatre into schools in the dual capacity of teachers and performers. Their recent play, *Radical Will*, developed in rehearsal and improvisation and, finally, scripted by their director, Claudia Leaf, includes so many examples of moving from the known to the unknown that it is reproduced here in its entirety. If we really believe that drama reflects and that the actors **are** "the abstract and brief chronicles of the time" then we, as teachers and leaders, must be prepared to engage with all the current issues which are of significance to our students as the creators of *Radical Will* have.

ℛadical Will

Claudia Leaf

Scripted for 13-14 year olds by Channel Theatre Company

Leanne: A young schoolgirl
Will: William Shakespeare, transplanted to the 1990s

There is no scenery. Leanne uses the space available to represent her own school hall - where she is practising a speech from A Midsummer Night's Dream, *soon to be performed in a workshop production by her class.*

Leanne *(Holding a script, comes to front)*:
"How happy some . . . oo-er . . . oh-ere . . ?"
(Looks at footnotes.) O'er? "O'er is one example of a word abbreviated to help the flow of the language. It is a shortened version of **over**." *(Angrily.)* Over! That's right! Take an easy little word like 'over' and write it so's no-one can understand it!
"How happy some o'er other some can be!
Through Athens I am thought as fair as she.
But what of that? Demetrius thinks not so;
He will not know what all but he do know.
He - will - not - know - what - all - but - he - do - know?"

(She repeats it again, quickly, then again with a different inflection, then shrugs as if she has still failed to grasp the meaning.)
  "And as he ears . . . errs . . . dotting on Hermia's eyes,
    So I, admiring of his qualities,"
"Dotting?" *(She looks at notes again.)* Dotting . . . dotting . . .
Oh, "Do-ting: Helena uses this word to make Demetrius'
love for Hermia seem silly and unimportant." Oh, yeah,
that's obvious really. **Not!** I need a drink! *(Opens school bag
and removes a soft drink. Drinks, then talks direct to audience.)*
I don't wanna be here, you know. I'd rather be at home,
watching *Home and Away* with a packet of chips in the
microwave. But I gotta learn my lines: it's impossible at
home with me brother Terry bursting into my room every
five minutes. We got a class production of *A Midsummer
Night's Dream* next Thursday - in front of the whole school.
It's really gross . . . but Miss Patel keeps telling us it'll only
be embarrassing if **we're** embarrassed. Well, I can guaran-
tee, **I'll** be embarrassing. My friend Kayleigh's OK, though.
She really makes me laugh. She's playing Hermia and it's all
I can do not to crease up when she acts. She reads it in this
posh voice, like that actress on the BBC video, and Miss Patel
says "Well done," but Kayleigh hasn't got a clue what she's
reading, either. She thinks it's a load of rubbish, like me. Oh
well, here goes.
  "Things base and vile, holding no quantity,
  Love can transpose to form and dignity
  *Will enters through a door and approaches Leanne,
  without being noticed, during the rest of the speech.*
  Love looks not with the eyes, but with the mind;
  And therefore is wing'd Cupid painted blind.
  Nor hath love's mind of any judgement taste;
  Wings and no eyes figure unheedy haste;
  And therefore is love said to be a child,
  Because in choice he is so oft beguil'd.
  As waggish boys themselves in game forswear
  So the boy love is perjur'd everywhere;
  For ere Demetrius look'd on Hermia's eyne

He hail'd down oaths that he was only mine;
And when this hail some heat from Hermia felt,
So he dissolv'd, and show'rs of oaths did melt."
Will *(Applauds sarcastically and encourages audience to join in)*:
Very good. Do you do *Yellow Pages* for an encore?
Leanne: What? Who are you?
Will: Or perhaps I could ask you to perform the Gillingham to Victoria railway timetable? Guaranteed to get everyone up on their feet, yelling for more.
Leanne: Were you listening to me?
Will: Couldnt help it.
Leanne: You could! You could've turned around and gone right back the way you came! You've got no right, creeping round here.
Will: I have, as a matter of fact.
Leanne: Oh, yeah? Since when?
Will*(Thinking)***:** Since about 1694, I suppose.
Leanne: You're crazy. I'm not staying here!
*Leanne goes to leave and **Will** catches her arm.*
Will: No, no! Don't go, I'm just having a bad day. I didn't mean to scare you.
Leanne: Well, you did.
Will: Sorry. Can I stay and watch?
Leanne: Watch what?
Will: You. What you were doing just now.
Leanne: No! I'm rehearsing for our class play!
Will: I don't mind! I'll be dead quiet - you won't know I'm here. Well, almost . . .
Leanne: You're kidding! You can't expect me to say this stuff with you standing there?!
Will: Why not?
Leanne: 'Cos I refuse to read this pile of shhh . . . well, you know . . . with you watching.
Will: What were you going to call your script just then?
Leanne: Nothing!
Will: Pile of **sh**aving foam? Pile of **sh**erbert lemons? Pile of ...
Leanne: No! I don't know what I was going to call it, all right?

Will: OK, OK.

Leanne: Good. Look, I wasn't getting at **you**. It's just these . . . these . . . **words**.

Will *(Looking over her shoulder)*: Which ones in particular?

Leanne: All of them! There's just too many.

Will *(With mock sympathy)*: Yeah, I can see . . .

Leanne: And I've got to learn them all by Thursday.

Will: Hard lines, Leanne . . .

Leanne: Yeah, and do you know . . . *(she realises what he has just said)* Now, wait a minute, how do you know my name?

Will *(Shrugging)*: Call it intuition.

Leanne: Look, I don't like this. Why are you here?

Will: Because I wrote it.

Leanne: Wrote what? What do you mean?

Will *(Taking the script from her)*: This. This pile of sheep's brains. This pile of shhh . . .

Leanne: All right! All right! I'm sorry I said it. So you **like** Shakespeare - how was I to know?

Will: No, I don't **like** him, I **am** him. There's a difference. Or maybe there isn't . . .

Leanne: What are you talking about? How could you be Shakespeare? Look, I don't know what you're on, but I'm getting out of here, right now.

*Leanne goes to leave but **Will** blocks her way.*

Will: I could help you, you know.

Leanne: I don't think so.

Will: I know you want to do it right.

Leanne: Oh, do you? Excuse me!

Will: So Danny Patteshall will fancy **you** instead of Joanne Riceman.

Leanne *(Stopping dead in her tracks)*: How do you know about Danny?

Will: I know a lot of things . . . I know Joanne got top marks last year for English. I know she's playing Titania in *A Midsummer Night's Dream* and she's wearing the dress her mother wore to the Fire Station's annual barbecue, but she had to take it in because Mrs. Riceman's a size fourteen. I know

Danny's playing Oberon, although he says he'd rather eat one of the rats in the Science Lab., and he's planning to ask Joanne out next Saturday . . . Do you want me to go on?

Leanne: No! Yes . . . I mean, you **can't**! You can't know all that!

Will: Well, I do.

Leanne: How?

Will: Nothing changes. That's the trouble with being four hundred and thirty-two years old. People are people, wherever you go. Same situations - just the clothes change. I think I've kept up with fashion OK. Don't you?

Leanne: Yeah, I suppose so. Nice trainers.

Will: Thanks.

Leanne: So how do you know about Danny?

Will: I watch people. So should you.

Leanne: He's gone all soft about Joanne. I hate her, she thinks she's so great with that ring in her belly button. She's nothing special. All my friends say I'm just as good-looking as she is. He just can't see it, that's all.

Will: "How happy some o'er other some can be . . ."

Leanne: Pardon?

Will: "Through Mulholland Park School I am thought as fair as
she,
But what of that? Danny Patteshall thinks not so.
He will not know what all but he do know."

Leanne: You're joking! Is that what it means?

Will: Yup.

Leanne: Is that what she's saying - Helena - about someone she fancies?

Will: Demetrius.

Leanne: And he fancies this other girl . . .

Will: Joanne - sorry! Hermia. Yes.

Leanne: And he's ignoring her?

Will: That's about the size of it.

Leanne: So why couldn't Miss just tell us that, instead of making us read all these notes?

Will: Search me.

Leanne: So what's all this stuff about Cupid having no eyes?

Will: She says if Cupid, God of Love, is blind, then Demetrius must be blind too: he sees with his mind and not his eyes. That's why he can't see what a dog Hermia really is!

Leanne *(Seeing the joke)*: You're kidding? That's really funny!

Will: Thanks.

Leanne: And what else?

Will: After that, Helena decides that a mind in love - particularly Demetrius' mind - isn't particularly cool, either. Like Cupid, who rushes around blindly with wings and no eyes.

Leanne: I don't think Danny's got a mind at the moment... not a proper, grown-up one, anyway.

Will: You mean he's behaving like a kid?

Leanne: Yeah! He really is!

Will: That's what Helena thinks about Demetrius:
"And therefore is Love said to be a child
Because in love he is so oft beguil'd."

Leanne: I don't believe this! It's weird.

Will: I thought it was OK. I really worked on that line: you wouldn't believe how many words rhyme with "child": mild, smiled, wild, filed ...

Leanne: No, I don't mean the rhyme! I mean the speech. It's just like what is going on with me right now ...

Will: So, try it again.

Leanne: What?

Will: Do it again! Think of Danny whilst you're doing it.

Leanne: I can't!

Will: You can!

Leanne: I don't want to do it in front of you.

Will: Perhaps I should remind you that you'll have the whole school watching you on Thursday.

Leanne: Don't!!! *(She goes to speak, then stops.)* It's no good! I can't do it!

Will: Then it's a good thing I came prepared.

Leanne: Pardon? *(Will rummages in his bag and brings out a "New Age" crystal on a thong and places it on Leanne's head.)* What are you doing?

Will: I'm activating the part of your brain which affects your self-confidence. It works every time. The crystal was given to me by these three old hags I met on holiday in Scotland. *(Pause.)* All right?

Leanne: Yeah! I feel better! This is really cool! I feel like I could do anything!

Will: Go on, then.

Leanne gives a blistering version of Helena's speech, investing it with the emotion she feels for Danny. Will applauds at end.

Leanne: That's weird! It all makes sense!

Will: I know.

Leanne: And I believe you now! You've gotta be who you say you are!

Will: I am.

Leanne: It's incredible. So, how does it feel to be four hundred and thirty-two years old?

Will: It's . . . interesting.

Leanne: Excuse me asking, but how do you manage to stay so . . . young-looking?

Will *(In pseudo-American accent)*: Because my work is still as fresh today as it was four hundred years ago, because every time my words are spoken, all over the world, my youth is returned to me again . . .

Leanne: Really?

Will: No, I'm kidding! I did a deal with the three witches.

Leanne: Which three witches?

Will: The three old hags I was talking about. In Scotland. They were witches.

Leanne: And?

Will: We did a deal. They knew I was a playwright, I knew they were into fame. So I promised to put them into one of my plays.

Leanne: So what did you get in return?

Will: The words of a spell, to put in a script. Every time that play is performed on stage, I get a little bit younger.

Leanne: But how did you know that it would still be performed, hundreds of years later?

Will: There was a fair chance. I made it a really bloody thriller: kings being slaughtered; mothers and children murdered. Then there's a supernatural prediction; an evil woman intent on murder who goes mad. Who could resist all that stuff in one play?

Leanne: I read a Point Horror that was a little bit like that last week . . .

Will: There you are, then. No-one can resist a bit of blood and gore. It was a smash hit . . . it ran and ran.

Leanne: And still does?

Will: Exactly.

Leanne: What's it called?

Will: *Macbeth*.

Leanne: We're not studying that. Wish we were. I'm sick of all these cutesy, little fairies in *A Midsummer Night's Dream*.

Will: Excuse me, but *The Dream's* fairies aren't like that.

Leanne: Like what?

Will: You know - all frilly and naff. In **my** time, fairies were taken seriously. They could do you good, but they could also do you a lot of harm. They could rule people's lives: spoil your crops; make your children ugly; send a flood to wreck your house - if you didn't show them Respect.

Leanne: So, did you know some fairies . . . like you met the witches?

Leanne: Er, Leanne . . . there's no such thing as fairies.

Leanne: But you just said!

Will: The poor people believed in them. It made a good excuse to blame the fairies when things went wrong.

Leanne: So Titania and Oberon are just made up?

Will: Not exactly. I used to hang out at the Queen's Court, remember. I saw enough royal tantrums . . .

Leanne: What was it like?

Will: Unreal. Like in *A Midsummer Night's Dream*. Being at court was like being in a play, only more unbelievable. Sometimes grand and dignified, sometimes full of petty squabbles - like the argument between Titania and Oberon. You should have heard some of the fights between Elizabeth and the Earl of Essex, poor guy. No wonder he ended up on the executioner's block!

Leanne: I did that in history. She fancied him, didn't she? Did they ever . . . you know?

Will: I'm not telling **you** that! But she certainly loved him at one time. She loved the theatre too, of course. We were always there, usually with a new show, whenever there was a big holiday or a festival to celebrate.

Leanne: Did you get to meet the Queen *just* for writing plays?

Will: I didn't *just* write plays - I was a **sensation**!

Leanne: Modest, too. So, a few people came to see your plays in that funny, round theatre of yours, and you got famous ...

Will: Not a *few*. Just about the whole of London. Look, have you heard of virtual reality?

Leanne: Course.

Will: What is it, then?

Leanne: Er, well . . . it's like cartoons that, er . . .

Will: It's computer-generated **life**, Leanne. You can experience spaces and places without ever setting foot in them. *(Will takes a virtual reality headset and glove from his bag.)* Now, put these on.

Leanne: No! What do they do?

Will: It's virtual reality. This is the helmet.

Leanne: I've never seen one of these. Where's the computer to run it?

Will: It's a portable version. Built it myself, programmed it myself. It's designed to take you back to my time. Put it on. And the glove.

Leanne: It's not dangerous, is it?

Will: No more than your telly. I'm switching it on now. What can you see?

Leanne: Nothing.

Will: Oh, it's not switched on. *(He flicks a switch on the helmet.)* That's better!

Leanne: Yeah! Cool! I can see it now. I'm outside, in a street, right next to the river. There are tall, wooden houses on either side . . . Urgh! What's that I'm walking in?

Will: Computer-generated sewage: it runs down the computer-generated streets, just like it used to in the olden days.

Leanne: Is the smell part of the experience?

Will: Yeah. Brilliant, isn't it?

Leanne: Not from where I'm breathing!

Will: Now what's happening?

Leanne: I'm turning a corner. The streets finish here. Up ahead there seems to be some open ground, like a field, and lots of trees. The houses look really run down here - there's a pub or something - a place selling drinks. Looks a bit rough to me. There's a gang of young guys hanging around outside.

Will: Good. That means you're going in the right direction for the Globe Theatre.

Leanne: What!? I thought your theatre was in a posh part of town!

Will: Not Southwark. Den of thieves. Whores, villains, pickpockets all hang out here.

Leanne: There's a man coming round the corner. Oh, my God! He's wearing tights!

Will: We all did then. It was cool.

Leanne: He's going to pass the men standing outside the pub. They're looking at him . . . they're whispering to each other. They're going after him . . . one of them's asking him something. For money, I think. He's smiling. He's shaking his head and walking on. They're going after him again . . . Oh, no! I don't believe this! One of them's got a knife . . . No! Look out!!!

Will (*Switching off the machine*): It's not real, you know.

Leanne (*Lifting off headset, shaken*): It could have been! What happens to the man in the programme?

Will: He defends himself with his sword. The gang leader loses an ear . . . and the others run off.

Leanne: Did you say he cut that guy's ear off? That's gross!

Will: It happens during the fight. We had to look after ourselves then: every gentleman carried a sword and a dagger. But don't go getting any ideas. They nick you for carrying offensive weapons, nowadays.

Leanne: Can I go back?

Will: If you want. *(He replaces headset.)* Now what do you see?

Leanne: I've moved further on, now, into the wooded part. Through the trees I can see some tall, round buildings. Like the Elizabethan theatres in Miss Patel's book. There's one very close, and one in the distance. There's hundreds of people swarming towards the far-off one. Some walking, some riding horses. It's a bit like a football crowd. There are so many people.

Will: Follow the crowd, Leanne. They're going in the right direction.

Leanne: I'm getting quite close to the first building. I'm walking past . . . Urgh! There's something in there - it stinks!

Will: Of what?

Leanne: I don't know. Like a zoo - or a butcher's shop.

Will: That'll be the Bear Garden. They bait bears - chain them up and set dogs on them - in there.

Leanne: It looks just like one of the other theatre buildings.

Will: Some of the theatres are used for plays **and** animal baiting, at different times. They just move the stage, but they never quite get rid of the smell of blood in the pit . . .

Leanne: I'm being pushed towards the bigger building: we're getting close to it. There's a flag flying, and a trumpet blowing from inside.

Will: Yeah, that means the performance is about to start.

Leanne: An afternoon performance?

Will: That's all we ever had. No electricity then, remember.

Leanne: Oh, yeah. We're going in. I'm in a dark passage, in a queue. Oh no, I'm outta here. They're gonna ask me for money in a minute and I've only got 25p!

Will: Just give the man at the gate anything round: the computer programme will convert it to an Elizabethan penny.

Leanne *(Feeling in her pockets)*: This feels like one of my little brother's Tazos - don't know what it's doing in here. Will that be OK?

Will: Yeah. Hand it over.

*Leanne blindly holds the Tazo out. **Will** takes and pockets it.*

Leanne: We're going inside now. Wow! It's big!

Will: Seats nearly two thousand people.

Leanne: We're standing in some sort of yard, and the stage is in front of us. It's amazing! The stage is really high up above me. And there're marble pillars!

Will: They're painted to **look** like marble.

Leanne: It's so **cool**! It's all done in golds and reds and blues! I thought Elizabethan theatres were just plain wood?

Will: Yes, but they were painted like palaces. Imagine a world where there's no television, no radio. Nothing to look at in the streets: no posters or billboards . . .

Leanne: No telly?

Will: . . . Then you pay a couple of pennies and step inside this theatre . . . and it's another world. Stories about kings and emperors; murders; battles and sword-fights. Romance, tragedy, disasters. It was all there . . .

Leanne: Shh! There's music playing - a sort of fanfare - and someone's coming on stage. The play's about to start . . . *(Will removes headset.)* What did you do that for?

Will: You wouldn't understand it.

Leanne: But you've just been telling me how easy your plays are to understand!

Will: No, I mean it would **sound** different: we spoke with a different accent then. It would sound like a foreign language to you.

Leanne: Well, that's my point. It's old English. That's why we can't follow it today.

Will: I'm only talking about the way it **sounded**: it's not so difficult to read on the page.

Leanne: Oh, here we go again! Look, it is to **me**! I may have just got the hang of *A Midsummer Night's Dream*, but I wouldn't read another of your plays if you paid me! Like *Julius Caesar* or *Henry V*. I mean, who wants to know about a load of old kings and emperors nowadays?

Will: Leanne - whether they're kings or emperors doesn't make any difference. I wrote about **people**. What audiences wanted then, and still do, is to recognise the people up there on the stage.

Leanne: You mean, like, see famous actors?

Will: No - I mean to see a character up on the stage and think, "That guy is just like my boss, or my neighbour, or the barman in the local pub." So they'd watch *Julius Caesar* and instead of all that history just going over their heads, people would say, "That Caesar's just like my boss - getting too pushy. I said the same things about him last week that Cassius is saying to Brutus." Or . . .

Leanne: Well, perhaps they did say that sort of thing **then**, but...

Will: They do now! *(He rummages in his bag and removes a book.)* Look at this scene from *Julius Caesar* . . .

Leanne: No, I haven't got time - I've gotta learn the rest of *A Midsummer Night's Dream* or Miss'll kill me . . .

Will: Look into the crytsal, Leanne. There's a little beam of coloured light, right in the middle. *(She looks.)* See?

Leanne: Yeah. Yeah - it's like a little rainbow. *(She reacts suddenly, as if she has briefly lost consciousness.)* I feel funny! Why did you make me do that?

Will: I implanted the words of the scene in your brain.

Leanne: You can do that?

Will: The crystal can do that, yeah.

Leanne: This is weird!

"Y'have ungently, Brutus,
Stole from my bed, and yesternight at supper . . . "

Oh! *(She clamps her hands over her mouth self-consciously.)* This is so bizarre! I can feel all these words in my head . . . Look, can you teach me the words to *A Midsummer Night's Dream* this way?

Will: I don't know . . .

Leanne: You must! You've got to! I'll do anything! What do I have to do?

Will: Let me take you through the scene, and I'll show you what I mean about making history real.

Leanne *(Reluctantly)*: If I must.

Will: You must. Now, think about those words in your head. What's happening?

Leanne: There's this girl . . . called Portia. She's dead upset about something. About her old man, Brutus. There's something big going on and he won't tell her what it is. She feels that he's in danger, but he's shutting her out . . .

Will: Yeah. That's it. I'll be Brutus. Let's do the scene. Leave me alone for a minute, then come in.

Leanne: OK. *(She "exits", returns as Portia.)* "Brutus, my Lord."

Will: "Portia! What mean you? Wherefore rise you now?
It is not for your health thus to commit
Your weak condition to the raw cold morning."

Leanne: "Nor for yours, neither. Y'have ungently, Brutus,
Stole from my bed; and yesternight at supper
You suddenly arose and walked about,
Musing and sighing, with your arms across;
And when I asked you what the matter was,
You stared upon me with ungentle looks."

She stops, obviously thinking of something else.

Will: What's the matter now?

Leanne: The scene. It reminds me of something.

Will: What?

Leanne: I dunno. Something I saw last night on telly.

Will: What was it? A historical documentary?

Leanne: No! No!! There was this guy, he was gonna do over an off-licence with his mates, and he was getting right jumpy about the thought of it. His girlfriend was trying to get the truth out of him, just like here, because she knew he was up to something.

Will: So what was the programme?

Leanne: It must have been one of the soaps. I don't watch anything else.

Will: OK. Tell me which one, and we'll do it like that.

Leanne: Like what?

Will: Like the TV show.

Leanne: You're joking, aren't you?

Will: Not in the least. Which one was it?

Leanne: Can't remember. I told you - I watch them all.

Will: Thank you. That's a great help. *(To audience.)* Give me the names of some soap operas.

He gets some large, blank pieces of card and pens, hands them out to audience and asks them to write the name of their favourite soap opera. He then shuffles the cards and asks a member of the audience to pick one out. The scene is then done in the style of the show on the chosen card. Key soaps are likely to be Neighbours; Home and Away; Hollyoaks; Eastenders; Brookside; Coronation Street. *In theory, the actors should be able to reproduce the scene as any one of these. A key prop, representative of the show, is used by* **Will** *in each case.*

Leanne: "Brutus, my Lord." *(She laughs.)* I can't do this. It's really cracking me up!

Will: Then I can't remember the spell for giving you Helena's lines in time for the performance.

Leanne: OK, OK, I'll do it. *(In character.)* "Brutus, my Lord."

Will: "Portia! What mean you? Wherefore rise you now?
It is not for your health thus to commit
Your weak condition to the raw cold morning."

Leanne: "Nor for yours, neither. Y'have ungently, Brutus,
Stole from my bed; and yesternight at supper
You suddenly arose and walked about,
Musing and sighing, with your arms across;
And when I asked you what the matter was,
You stared upon me with ungentle looks.
I urged you further; then you scratched your head,
And too impatiently stamped with your foot;
Yet I insisted, yet you answered not,
But with an angry wafture of your hand
Gave sign for me to leave you. So I did,
Fearing to strengthen that impatience
Which seemed too much enkindled, and withal
Hoping it was but an effect of humour,
Which sometime hath his hour with every man."
Hold on, how can "humour" make you bad-tempered?

Will: Four hundred years ago, the study of the 'humours' in the body was the latest thing in alternative medicine. Come to think of it, there **weren't** any alternatives.

Leanne: Oh. Now, where was I? Oh, yeah:
"It will not let you eat, nor talk, nor sleep;
And could it work so much upon your shape,
As it hath much prevailed on your condition,
I should not know you, Brutus. Dear my Lord,
Make me acquainted with your cause of grief."

Will: "I am not well in health, and that is all."

Leanne: "Brutus is wise, and were he not in health,
He would embrace the means to come by it."

Will: "Why, so I do. *(Shows her aspirin box.)*
Good Portia, go to bed."

Leanne: "Is Brutus sick? And is it physical
To walk unbraced and suck up the humours
Of the dank morning? What, is Brutus sick?
And will he steal out of his wholesome bed
To dare the vile contagion of the night,
And tempt the rheumy and unpurged air,
To add unto his sickness? No, my Brutus;
You have some sick offence within your mind
Which, by the right and virtue of my place,
I ought to know of; and, upon my knees,
I charm you, by my once commended beauty,
By all your vows of love, and that great vow
Which did incorporate and make us one,
That you unfold to me, your self, your half,
Why you are heavy, and what men tonight
Have had resort to you; for here have been
Some six or seven, who did hide their faces
Even from darkness."

Will: "Kneel not, gentle Portia."

Leanne: "I should not kneel if you were gentle Brutus.
Within the bond of marriage, tell me, Brutus,
Is it excepted I should know no secrets
That appertain to you? Am I your self

But, as it were, in sort or limitation,
To keep with you at meals, comfort your bed,
And talk to you sometimes? Dwell I but in the suburbs
Of your good pleasure? If it be no more,
Portia is Brutus' harlot, not his wife."
Leanne starts to exit, **Will** *pulls her back.*
Will: "You are my true and honourable wife,
As dear to me as are the ruddy drops
That visit my sad heart."
Leanne: "If this were true, then should I know this secret.
I grant I am a woman; but withal
A woman that Lord Brutus took to wife;
I grant I am a woman; but withal
A woman well reputed, Cato's daughter.
Think you I am no stronger than my sex,
Being so fathered, and so husbanded?
Tell me your counsels, I will not disclose 'em.
I have made strong proof of my constancy,
Giving myself a voluntary wound
Here, in the thigh."
She lifts her skirt to reveal a tattoo. Audience should laugh.
If they do not, **Will** *does.*

Well, what's so funny about a tattoo? It hurts like hell,
having it done, I can tell you. That's the sort of thing you'd
do to prove you loved someone, isn't it?
Will: What does yours say?
Leanne*(Pulling skirt down)*: Never you mind.
Will: Good. Well, at least you're getting the hang of it.
Leanne: So, what was Brutus going to do?
Will: Assassinate Julius Caesar. Don't you know anything
about history?
Leanne: He doesn't seem like a murderer.
Will: It would be good if assassins wore little badges saying,
"Killing is fun. Have a nice day." But they don't. That's how
people get murdered. Brutus is just an ordinary man - he just
makes an extraordinary decision: to kill his ruler.

Leanne: And he doesn't tell his wife about it?

Will: No.

Leanne: Yeah, he **is** an ordinary man.

Will: Brutus might be an important historical figure, but he had the same feelings as you or I. We're talking about out-of-the-ordinary, world-shattering events here, but they're carried out by ordinary people. Like Julius Caesar: since he was so famous, I had to work against making him into some unreal **legend**. I tried to show he was weak - he cries out to Cassius for help when he loses a race across the River Tiber and a fever he catches in Spain makes him groan and cry out for water like a child. And he's arrogant. He ignores his wife's dreams **and** the soothsayer's predictions . . .

Leanne: Yeah, yeah. OK.

Will: So?

Leanne: So what?

Will: So, isn't it better to make **drama** work for people? Make history come alive, so we can all learn something about our own lives from it? Don't you think that's important?

Leanne: I dunno.

Will: Leanne . . .

Leanne: Yeah?

Will: I'm not getting through to you, am I?

Leanne: Yeah, you are. I know what you're saying. It's what Miss Patel says, too. It's just what I'd expect you to say, if you really were Shakespeare.

Will: The trouble is, you're looking at me as I am now, but you're still seeing a bald-headed git in tights, scratching on a piece of parchment with a quill pen.

Leanne: No I'm not! I hadn't really thought about you at all before . . .

Will: I've had to put up with this for hundreds of years, you know!! This attitude that I'm just a piece of England's heritage, like Stonehenge or the Houses of Parliament!

Leanne: Why, what's wrong with that?

Will: In my time, I was a ground-breaker . . . an innovator . . . I was even condemned for being a bad moral influence! Did you know that when we performed at The Globe, we wore modern dress? I used stories that were well-known, but I brought them right up to date. The audiences loved it: the authorities tried to throw us out of town.

Leanne: You're kidding!

Will: It's true! The guys who ran the City of London hated us. They said we were a bad influence on young people, and they were always looking for an excuse to shut the playhouses down. So we went on tour when we couldn't work in London. We played in pubs, in rich people's houses - anywhere we could raise a crowd.

Leanne: So you didn't work in The Globe Theatre all the time?

Will: Not in the summer, when there was plague around. Then they'd shut us down.

Leanne: You mean to stop people passing on infection?

Will: That was one of the reasons. The real reason was that they thought we were dangerous.

Leanne: So they thought you were dangerous, did they? I don't believe it. Wait till I tell Kayleigh!

Will: Tell Kayleigh what?

Leanne: Shakespeare - a bad influence on young people!

Will: Well, I was!

Leanne: Still are! I get a terrible headache reading all that poetry!

Will (*Annoyed*): I don't see what's so wrong with poetry! It was the way we all wrote then.

Leanne: Yeah, but that doesn't mean we have to like it now.

Will: But if . . . .

Leanne: I mean, take *Romeo and Juliet*. Miss brought in a video the other day and made us watch it. All that "what light through yonder window breaks?" stuff. I **mean**, what kind of sad anorak would say that to a girl he fancies on their first date?

Will: I thought it was more romantic than some of Danny's chat-up lines. "Oh, you've got really nice eyes, Joanne," doesn't really get me reaching for the Kleenex somehow.

Leanne: Did he say that?

DRAMA IMPROVISED

Will: No. Can't you take a joke?

Leanne: Oh, you pig! *(She goes to hit him, but he ducks.)* Just because I'm right, and you know it. Teachers always think *Romeo and Juliet* has got to mean something to us, because it's about two young people who fall in love. But it's rubbish. You can't feel any sympathy for them because they're so **useless**: they should have told their parents where to go and run away and got married.

Will: You got a passport?

Leanne: No.

Will: Pity.

Leanne: Why?

Will: I was going to book you on a flight to Chechnya.

Leanne: Isn't that the country that was at war with Russia? Why would I want to go there?

Will: To learn a few home truths, Leanne. There are still places in the world where families have complete power over their children: enough to stop them marrying. *(To audience.)* Give me some examples of countries at war. *(Look for Northern Ireland, Cyprus/Turkey, Hutus/Tutsis, Kurds in Iraq and Turkey, possibly the black/white conflict.)* And if your parents are Serbs living in Bosnia, and you're fourteen and in love with a Croat boy, then they won't let you marry him, and you can't run away. There's no-one and nowhere to run to. You can't be with him, and you'd never survive on your own. It was like that in Verona, where Romeo and Juliet lived.

Leanne: OK, so maybe they didn't have a lot of choice about that. But they could've cut out all that poetry and spoken like real people.

Will: Why has it got to be so "real"?

Leanne: 'Cos otherwise I don't believe it.

Will: So everything's got to be in black and white, has it?

Leanne: What do you mean?

Will: There's no room in that head of yours for an idea that may be bigger than real life?

Leanne: What? Look, don't start on me again! All I know is what I like and don't like . . .

Will: All I'm asking is that you just open your eyes to what words can do! Look, you mentioned "what light through yonder window breaks?" Now, if you remember, Romeo goes on to say "It is the east, and Juliet is the sun."

Leanne: Yeah, well, she's not the sun, is she? That's just stupid.

Will: No, she's not the sun, but to Romeo she's **like** the sun. *(If the audience is friendly, this should be addressed to them.)* What does the sun do? Yeah, it lights up the sky. It makes things grow. It brings life. That's what Juliet does for Romeo. For him, she lights up a room when she walks into it. She makes him feel alive, in fact she's all his feelings about life and hope. So, she's his sun, the real 'light of his life.'

Leanne: You don't half go on.

Will: That's exactly my point! It's quicker to say "Juliet is the sun" than to list all the feelings Romeo has about her. We all get the idea faster.

Leanne: That Balcony Scene's so . . . **pathetic**. People today don't talk like that when they're in love.

Will: Leanne, look into the crystal.

Leanne: Are you going to give me the *Midsummer Night's Dream* lines now?

Will: That's right. Just relax and watch the crystal, Leanne. *(He swings it like a pendulum - hypnotising her.)* You're feeling heavy, heavy, heavy . . . good. Now, sleep! *(Her head drops to one side.)* Now, when you wake up, you'll not only know all Juliet's lines, you'll look at me - as Romeo - and see Danny Patteshall standing there. You're going to find out that people in love have been acting the same way since the beginning of time - let alone four hundred years ago.

Let me give you some background. You've just been to a school disco, but it was bad news. You've just discovered that Danny is the son of your Father's greatest enemy, Gary Patteshall, who runs the rival window-cleaning business in town. He and your Dad haven't spoken since Gary greased your Father's ladder with cholesterol-free cooking-oil, eight years ago! It's late at night. You're standing on your parents' patio. Danny's out there somewhere . . . walking up the High

83

Street, maybe; or waiting for a portion of chips at *Harry's Fish Bar* . . . thinking of you.

Leanne: "Oh, Daniel! Daniel! Wherefore art thou, Daniel?
Deny thy father and refuse thy name
Or if though will not, be but sworn my love
And I'll no longer be Leanne McTeill."

Will: "Shall I hear more, or shall I speak at this?"

Leanne: "'Tis but thy name which is my enemy;
Thou art thyself, though not a Patteshall.
What's Patteshall? It is nor hand, nor foot,
Nor arm, nor face, nor any other part
Belonging to a man. O, be some other name!
What's in a name? That which we call a rose
By any other name would smell as sweet;
So Daniel would, were he not Daniel call'd,
Retain that dear perfection which he owes
Without that title. Daniel, doff thy name;
And for thy name, which is no part of thee,
Take all myself."

Will: "I take thee at thy word;
Call me but love, and I'll be new baptis'd:
Henceforth I never will be Daniel."

Leanne: "What man art thou, that, thus bescreen'd in night,
So stumblest on my counsel?"

Will: "By a name,
I know not how to tell thee who I am:
My name, dear saint, is hateful to myself
Because it is an enemy to thee;
Had I it written, I would tear the word."

Leanne: "My ears have not yet drunk a hundred words
Of thy tongue's uttering, yet I know the sound:
Art thou not Daniel, and a Patteshall?"

Will: "Neither, fair maid, if either thee dislike."

Leanne: "How cam'st thou hither, tell me, and wherefore?
The orchard walls are high and hard to climb;
And the place death, considering who thou art,
If any of my kinsmen find thee here."

Will: "With love's light wings did I o'erperch these walls,
For stony limits cannot hold love out;
And what love can do, that dares love attempt.
Therefore their kinsmen are no stop to me."
Leanne: "If they do see thee, they will murder thee."
Will: "Alack, there lies more peril in thine eye
Than twenty of their swords; look thou but sweet,
And I am proof against their enmity."
Leanne: "I would not for the world they saw thee here."
Will: "I have night's cloak to hide me from their eyes;
And but thou love me, let them find me here.
My life were but ended with their hate
Than death prorogued wanting of thy love."
Leanne: "By whose direction found'st thou out this place?"
Will: "By love, that first did prompt me to enquire;
He lent me counsel, and I lent him eyes.
I am no pilot; yet, wert thou as far
As that vast shore wash'd with the farthest sea
I should adventure for such merchandise."
Leanne: "Thou knowest the mask of night is on my face
Else would a maiden blush bepaint my cheek
For that which thou hast heard me speak tonight.
Fain would I swell on form, fain, fain deny
What I have spoke; but farewell compliment!
Dost thou love me? I know thou wilt say ay,
And I will take thy word; yet if thou swear'st,
Thou mayst prove false; at lovers' perjuries
They say Jove laughs. O gentle Daniel,
If thou dost love, pronounce it faithfully.
Or, if thou thinkst I am too quickly won,
I'll frown, and be perverse, and say thee nay,
So thou wilt woo; but else, not for the world.
In truth, fair Patteshall, I am too fond;
And therefore thou mayst think my haviour light;
But trust me, gentleman, I'll prove more true
Than those that have more cunning to be strange.
I should have been more strange, I must confess

But that thou overheard'st, ere I was ware,
My true love's passion. Therefore pardon me,
And not impute this yielding to light love,
Which the dark night have so discovered."

Will: "Lady, by yonder blessed moon I vow,
That tips with silver all these fruit-tree tops - "

Leanne: "O, swear not by the moon, th'inconstant moon,
That monthly changes in her circled orb,
Lest that thy love prove likewise variable."

Will: "What shall I swear by?"

Leanne: "Do not swear at all;
Or if thou wilt, swear by thy gracious self,
Which is the god of my idolatry,
And I'll believe thee."

Will: "If my heart's dear love - "

Leanne: "Well, do not swear. Although I joy in thee,
I have no joy of this contract tonight.
It is too rash, too unadvis'd, too sudden:
Too like the lightning, which doth cease to be
Ere one can say "It lightens". Sweet, good night!
This bud of love, by summer's ripening breath,
May prove a beauteous flow'r when next we meet.
Good night! Good night! As sweet repose and rest
Come to thy heart as that within my breast!"

Will: "O, wilt thou leave me so unsatisfied?"

Leanne: "What satisfaction canst thou have tonight?"

Will: "Th'exchange of thy love's faithful vow for mine."

Leanne: "I gave thee mine before thou didst request it;
And yet I would it were to give again."

Will: "Would'st thou withdraw it? For what purpose, love?"

Leanne: "But to be frank, and give it thee again.
And yet I wish but for the thing I have.
My bounty is as boundless as the sea,
My love as deep; the more I give to thee,
The more I have, for both are infinite.
(Will claps his hands to bring her out of trance.)
I hear some noise within. I . . . I . . . "

RADICAL WILL

Leanne staggers and wakes. She is clearly upset.
She sits, with her head in her hands.

Will: What is it?

Leanne: Nothing. Nothing! I must've dropped off, just then. I...I had this dream. About Danny. He was... I don't know. It's just he never ...

Will: Never talked to you like that before?

Leanne: Yeah. How did you know?

Will: A guess. I heard you talking in your sleep. What else happened in your dream?

Leanne: Nothing. He was just there, in our garden, and he was in danger, and he said these **things** ...

Will: What things?

Leanne: I'm not telling you! It was private.

Will: Oh, I see.

Leanne: It was wonderful.

Will: Good.

Leanne: You know, sometimes when you get caught up in a dream and it's more real ... more real than ... *(she searches for the right words)* ...

Will: Than real life?

Leanne: Yeah. Yeah ... *(she puts her head in her hands)* that's it.

Will: So, what's the matter now?

Leanne: I didn't want it to end. Why did I have to wake up?

Will: Because no matter how enjoyable the dream, we all have to wake up and face reality in the end. Remember *A Midsummer Night's Dream*?

Leanne: Yeah. I suppose so.

Will: Well, time I was going. *(He holds the crystal against her head. She reacts as if it is slightly painful.)* There, that's Helena taken care of. All right?

Leanne: Yeah. Thanks.

Will: Do you know another thing those witches taught me?

Leanne: What?

Will: I can see into the future. I know you'll be terrific on Thursday.

Leanne: Ta.

Will: And I know something else. Like who's waiting outside the gates, right now.

Leanne: What? Are you having me on?

Will: He's been there for the past half-hour. He's pretending to look at his script, but every few minutes he keeps glancing over to the hall: something tells me he's waiting for you.

Leanne: Oh, God! Danny! I don't believe it! *(To Will.)* Look, thanks a lot, but I gotta go!

Leanne exits and Will calls after her.

Will: I don't think he'll be making a night of it, Leanne. He's got to learn Acts Three and Four before tomorrow morning! *(He goes to his bag.)* So . . . where am I tomorrow? *(Says name of school where performance is actually taking place.)* Ah well, shouldn't take long - I'll need to get off early - my Theatre Listings web-site on the Net tells me there's a production of *Macbeth* opening in Glasgow tomorrow night. Only pub-theatre, of course, but it's got to be good for - what? one, two, three weeks younger? If the three witches' spell keeps going at this rate, I'll be signing myself up for Nursery School in about two years' time! Well, how was I supposed to know my work would be so popular!?

Will exits.

The End

This play, devised by Claudia Leaf with Channel Theatre's T.I.E. Company, is used by permission of Channel Theatre.

No performance fee is payable for classroom use, but fees are applicable if a public performance is given.

The script is also published separately by:

J. Garnet Miller Limited

Bibliography

Education and Theatre

Allen, J. *Drama in Schools: Its Theory and Practice*, Heinemann, 1979

Billington, M. *The Life and Work of Harold Pinter*, Faber & Faber, 1996

Boagey, E. *Starting Drama*, Belland Hyman, 1986

Boal, A. *The Theatre of the Oppressed*, T.C.G. Books, 1992

Boal, A. *Games for Actors and Non-Actors*, Routledge, 1992

Bolton, G. *Towards a Theory of Drama in Education*, Longman, 1979

Hilton, F. *The Vocabulary of Educational Drama*, Kemble Press, 1973

Hodgson, J. & Richards, E. *Improvisation*, Eyre Methuen, 1974

Johnstone, K. *Impro: Improvisation and the Theatre*, Eyre Methuen, 1981

Koste, V. *Dramatic Play in Early Childhood*, Un'ty Press America, 1987

Lamont, G. *English: Speaking and Listening*, John Murray, 1995

MacGregor, L., et al. *Learning through Drama*, Heinemann, 1977

Male, D. *Approaches to Drama*, Allen and Unwin, 1973

Marowitz, C. *Recycling Shakespeare*, Macmillan, 1991

O'Neill, M., et al. *Drama Guidelines*, Heinemann, 1976

Pemberton-Billing & Clegg, D. *Teaching Drama*, Un'ty London P, 1965

Pickering, K. *How to Study Modern Drama*, Macmillan, 1986

Pickering, K., et al. *Investigating Drama*, Allen and Unwin, 1974

Robinson, K. (Ed.). *Exploring Theatre and Education*, Heinemann, 1980

Ross, M. *The Creative Arts*, Heinemann, 1978

DRAMA IMPROVISED

Slade, P. *Child Drama*, U.L.P. (UK), Verry Laurence (US), 1954
Stabler, T. *Drama in Primary Schools*, Macmillan, 1979
Stanislavsky, C. *Creating a Rôle*, Bles (UK), Mentor (US), 1936
Wagner, B. *Dorothy Heathcote: Drama as a Learning Medium*, Hutchinson,
1979

Drama Therapy

Amies, B., Warren, B. & Watling, R. *Social Drama*, John Clare, 1986
Boal, A. *Games for Actors and Non-Actors*, Routledge, 1992
Gale, D. *What is Psychodrama? A Personal and Practical Guide*, Gale, '90
Gersie, A. & King, N. *Storymaking in Education and Therapy*, Kingsley,
1990
Grainger, R. *Drama and Healing: The Roots of Dramatherapy*, Kingsley,
1990
Holmes, P. & Karp, M. (Ed.). *Psychodrama: Inspiration and Technique*,
Tavistock-Routledge, 1991
Jennings, S *Creative Drama: Groupwork*, Winslow, 1986
Jennings, S. (Ed.). *Dramatherapy: Theory and Practice for Teachers
and Clinicians*, Routledge, 1987
Jennings, S. (Ed.) *Dramatherapy: Theory and Practice 2*,
Tavistock/Routledge, 1992
Landy, R. *Drama Therapy: Concept and Practices*, Charles Thomas, 1986
McCaughan, N. & Scott, T. *Rôle Play and Simulation Games*,
National Institute of Social Work, 1978
Schutzman, M. & Cohen-Cruz, J. *Playing Boal: Theatre, Therapy,
Activism*, Routledge, 1994
Warren, B. (Ed.). *Using the Creative Arts in Therapy*, Routledge, 1993

Plays

Arden, J. *Happy Haven*, Penguin (UK), Grove (US)
Ayckbourn, A. *Ernie's Incredible Illucinations*, Samuel French
Beckett, S. *Waiting for Godot*, Faber (UK), Grove Evergreen (US)
Brecht, B. *The Caucasian Chalk Circle*, Methuen (UK), Grove (US)
Life of Galileo, Methuen (UK), Grove (US)
Campton, D. *The Cage Birds*, French (UK), Dramatic Publishing (US)
Smile, French (UK), Dramatic Publishing (US)
Clark, B. *Campion's Interview*, (unpublished TV script)
Donleavy, J.P. *The Interview*, in *Theatre Today*, Longman
Eliot, T.S. *Murder in the Cathedral*, Faber

BIBLIOGRAPHY

Godber, J *Bouncers*
Harrison, T. *The Mysteries*, Faber
Huxley, A. *The Gioconda Smile*, Samuel French
Mankowitz, W. *It Should Happen to a Dog*, in *Theatre Today*, Longman
Miller, A. *A View from the Bridge*, Penguin, Cresset (UK), Viking (US)
Mortimer, J. *Dock Brief*, Samuel French
O'Neill, E. *In the Zone*, Cape (UK), Random House (US)
Pickering, K. *Beowulf*, Samuel French (UK), I.E. Clark (US)
   The Ingoldsby Legends, J. Garnet Miller
   The Midlands Mystery Plays at Birmingham, J. Garnet Miller
   Turtle Island, One World Publications
Pinter, H. *The Dumb Waiter*, French (UK), Dramatic Publishing (US)
   The Caretaker, French (UK), Dramatic Publishing (US)
Rattigan, T. *The Winslow Boy*, Longman
Rook, R. *Play Ten*, Hutchinson
Sartre, J.P *In Camera* (or *No Exit*) [*Huis Clos*], Penguin (UK), French (US)
   Men without Shadows (*Mort sans Sepultures*), Penguin (UK),
                    French (US)
   The Flies (*Les Mouches*), Penguin (UK), Knopf (US)
Sellar and Yeatman. *1066 and All That*, Samuel French
Shaffer, P. *The Royal Hunt of the Sun*, Hamish Hamilton
Shakespeare, W. (No particular edition is recommended as there are
now many attractive and accurate texts):
   A Midsummer Night's Dream
   Macbeth
   Julius Caesar
   The Merchant of Venice
   Hamlet
   The Tempest
Simpson, N.F. *One Way Pendulum*, Faber

Other Sources

Dates and publishers of classics available in many editions are not
included.

Books

Aesop *Fables*
Alcott, Louisa M. *Little Women* (dramatisations also available)
Bullfinch, T. *The Age of Fable*, Everyman (UK) Collier Macmillan (US)
Bunyan, John. *The Pilgrim's Progress*
Dickens, Charles. *Great Expectations*
    A Tale of Two Cities
    The Pickwick Papers
Fitzgerald, F. Scott. *The Diamond as Big as the Ritz*, Penguin (UK),
    Scribner (US)
Golding, William. *Lord of the Flies*, Penguin/Faber (UK), Putnam (US)
Great Fights in Literature, Various authors, Dent
Haggard, Rider. *King Solomon's Mine*
Hemingway, E. *For Whom the Bell Tolls*, Penguin (UK), Scribner (US)
Hughes, M.V. *A London Child of the 1870's*, OUP, 1934
Orwell, G. *1984*
    Animal Farm
Scott, Sir Walter, *Ivanhoe*
Sutcliff, R. *The Eagle of the Ninth*, OUP (UK), Walck (US)
Swift, J. *Gulliver's Travels*
Verne, J. *20,000 Leagues Under the Sea*
Warren, C.H. *A Boy in Kent*, Bles, 1937
Wells, H. G. *The History of Mr. Polly*
    The War of the Worlds
White, R.H. *The Sword in the Stone*
Williams, K. *Just William*

Poems and Sagas

Arnold, Matthew. *Balder Dead*
Coleridge, S.T. *The Rime of the Ancient Mariner*
Dante. *The Inferno*
Gibson, W.W. *Flannan Isle*
Homer. *The Odyssey*
    The Iliad